THE
SIGNET
WORLD
ATLAS

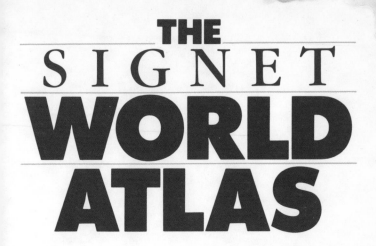

THE SIGNET WORLD ATLAS

B. M. Willett
Cartographic Editor

A SIGNET BOOK

SIGNET
Published by the Penguin Group
Penguin Books USA Inc., 375 Hudson Street,
New York, New York 10014, U.S.A.
Penguin Books Ltd, 27 Wrights Lane, London W8 5TZ, England
Penguin Books Australia Ltd, Ringwood, Victoria, Australia
Penguin Books Canada Ltd, 10 Alcorn Avenue,
Toronto, Ontario, Canada M4V 3B2
Penguin Books (N.Z.) Ltd, 182-190 Wairau Road,
Auckland 10, New Zealand

Penguin Books Ltd, Registered Offices:
Harmondsworth, Middlesex, England

First published by Signet, an imprint of New American Library,
a division of Penguin Books USA Inc. Previously published in a different edition in Great
Britain by George Philip, Limited.

First Signet Printing, October, 1991
10 9 8 7 6 5 4 3 2 1

Ⓙ REGISTERED TRADEMARK—MARCA REGISTRADA

Printed in Hong Kong

Books are available at quantity discounts when used to promote products or services.
For information please write to Premium Marketing Division, Penguin Books USA Inc.,
375 Hudson Street, New York, New York 10014.

CONTENTS

UNITED
STATES
AND WORLD
STATISTICS

UNITED STATES – STATES

Population 1990

	Total population	Rank	% of US Total	Density (Persons per Square mile)	Population Change 1980-1990
ALABAMA	4,062,608	22	1.6	80	3.9
ALASKA	551,947	50	0.2	1	37.3
ARIZONA	3,677,985	24	1.5	32	34.9
ARKANSAS	2,362,239	33	0.9	45	2.9
CALIFORNIA	29,839,250	1	12.0	190	25.7
COLORADO	3,307,912	26	1.3	32	14.0
CONNECTICUT	3,295,669	27	1.3	675	5.8
DELAWARE	668,696	46	0.3	345	11.9
D. OF COLUMBIA	609,909	48	0.2	9,633	-4.8
FLORIDA	13,003,362	4	5.2	239	32.8
GEORGIA	6,508,419	11	2.6	112	18.6
HAWAII	1,115,274	40	0.4	172	14.8
IDAHO	1,011,986	42	0.4	12	6.7
ILLINOIS	11,466,682	6	4.6	205	0.1
INDIANA	5,564,228	14	2.2	154	1.0
IOWA	2,787,424	30	1.1	50	-4.7
KANSAS	2,485,600	32	1.0	30	4.8
KENTUCKY	3,698,969	23	1.5	93	0.7
LOUISIANA	4,238,216	21	1.7	95	0.4
MAINE	1,233,223	38	0.5	40	9.2
MARYLAND	4,798,622	19	1.9	486	13.4
MASSACHUSETTS	6,029,051	13	2.4	769	4.9
MICHIGAN	9,328,784	8	3.7	163	0.4
MINNESOTA	4,387,029	20	1.8	55	7.3
MISSISSIPPI	2,586,443	31	1.0	54	2.1
MISSOURI	5,137,804	15	2.1	74	4.1
MONTANA	803,655	44	0.3	5	1.6
NEBRASKA	1,584,617	36	0.6	21	0.5
NEVADA	1,206,152	39	0.5	11	50.4
NEW HAMPSHIRE	1,113,915	41	0.4	123	20.5
NEW JERSEY	7,748,634	9	3.1	1,035	5.0
NEW MEXICO	1,521,779	37	0.6	12	16.5
NEW YORK	18,044,505	2	7.2	380	2.5
NORTH CAROLINA	6,657,630	10	2.7	136	12.8
NORTH DAKOTA	641,364	47	0.3	9	-2.1
OHIO	10,887,325	7	4.4	265	0.5
OKLAHOMA	3,157,604	28	1.3	46	4.0
OREGON	2,853,733	29	1.1	30	8.0
PENNSYLVANIA	11,924,710	5	4.8	265	0.1
RHODE ISLAND	1,005,984	43	0.4	951	5.9
SOUTH CAROLINA	3,505,707	25	1.4	115	11.8
SOUTH DAKOTA	699,999	45	0.3	3	0.8
TENNESSEE	4,896,641	17	2.0	119	6.2
TEXAS	17,059,805	3	6.8	65	19.4
UTAH	1,727,784	35	0.7	21	17.9
VERMONT	564,964	49	0.2	61	10.0
VIRGINIA	6,216,568	12	2.5	156	15.7
WASHINGTON	4,887,941	18	2.0	73	17.8
WEST VIRGINIA	1,801,625	34	0.7	74	-8.0
WISCONSIN	4,906,745	16	2.0	90	4.0
WYOMING	455,975	51	0.2	5	-3.7
UNITED STATES	**249,632,692**		**100**	**70**	**9.8**

The Total population is the Resident population plus persons who normally live in the state who were overseas at the time of the Census. The density of population has been calculated by dividing the Resident Population by the land area of the state, and not by the Total area shown to the right of the table, which includes inland water.

Residential Population 1990	Residential Population 1980	% of US Total 1980	Total Area Square Miles	Rank	
4,040,587	3,890,061	1.7	51,705	29	ALABAMA
550,043	400,481	0.2	591,004	1	ALASKA
3,665,228	2,717,866	1.2	114,000	6	ARIZONA
2,350,725	2,285,513	1.0	53,187	27	ARKANSAS
29,760,021	23,668,562	10.4	158,706	3	CALIFORNIA
3,294,394	2,888,834	1.3	104,091	8	COLORADO
3,287,116	3,107,576	1.4	5,018	48	CONNECTICUT
666,168	595,225	0.3	2,045	49	DELAWARE
606,900	637,651	0.3	69	51	D. OF COLUMBIA
12,937,926	9,739,992	4.3	58,664	22	FLORIDA
6,478,216	5,464,265	2.4	58,910	21	GEORGIA
1,108,229	965,000	0.4	6,471	47	HAWAII
1,006,749	943,935	0.4	83,564	13	IDAHO
11,430,602	11,418,461	5.0	56,345	24	ILLINOIS
5,544,159	5,490,179	2.4	36,185	38	INDIANA
2,776,755	2,913,387	1.3	56,275	25	IOWA
2,477,574	2,363,208	1.0	82,277	14	KANSAS
3,685,296	3,661,433	1.6	40,410	37	KENTUCKY
4,219,973	4,203,972	1.9	47,752	31	LOUISIANA
1,227,928	1,124,660	0.5	33,265	39	MAINE
4,781,468	4,216,446	1.9	10,460	42	MARYLAND
6,016,425	5,737,037	2.5	8,284	45	MASSACHUSETTS
9,295,297	9,258,344	4.1	58,527	23	MICHIGAN
4,375,099	4,077,148	1.8	84,402	12	MINNESOTA
2,573,216	2,520,638	1.1	47,689	32	MISSISSIPPI
5,117,073	4,917,444	2.2	69,697	19	MISSOURI
799,065	786,690	0.3	147,046	4	MONTANA
1,578,385	1,570,006	0.7	77,355	15	NEBRASKA
1,201,833	799,184	0.4	110,561	7	NEVADA
1,109,252	920,610	0.4	9,279	44	NEW HAMPSHIRE
7,730,188	7,364,158	3.3	7,787	46	NEW JERSEY
1,515,065	1,299,968	0.6	121,593	5	NEW MEXICO
17,990,455	17,557,288	7.8	49,108	30	NEW YORK
6,628,637	5,874,429	2.6	52,669	28	NORTH CAROLINA
638,800	652,695	0.3	70,702	17	NORTH DAKOTA
10,847,115	10,797,419	4.8	41,330	35	OHIO
3,145,585	3,025,266	1.3	69,956	18	OKLAHOMA
2,842,321	2,632,663	1.2	97,073	10	OREGON
11,881,643	11,866,728	5.2	45,308	33	PENNSYLVANIA
1,003,464	947,154	0.4	1,212	50	RHODE ISLAND
3,486,703	3,119,208	1.4	31,113	40	SOUTH CAROLINA
696,004	690,178	0.3	77,116	16	SOUTH DAKOTA
4,877,185	4,590,750	2.0	42,144	34	TENNESSEE
16,986,510	14,228,383	6.3	266,807	2	TEXAS
1,722,850	1,461,037	0.6	84,899	11	UTAH
562,758	511,456	0.2	9,614	43	VERMONT
6,187,358	5,346,279	2.4	40,767	36	VIRGINIA
4,866,692	4,130,163	1.8	68,139	20	WASHINGTON
1,793,477	1,949,644	0.9	24,232	41	WEST VIRGINIA
4,891,769	4,705,335	2.1	56,153	26	WISCONSIN
453,588	470,816	0.2	97,809	9	WYOMING
248,709,873	226,504,825	100	3,618,770		UNITED STATES

UNITED STATES – STATES

	Personal Income 1988	% of US Average 1988	Rank	- 5 Years 1985 %	5-17 Years 1985 %	+ 65 Years 1985 %	Population 1985 (Thousands)
ALABAMA	12,852	78	41	7.4	20.3	12.1	4,021
ALASKA	19,079	116	8	11.5	21.1	3.2	521
ARIZONA	14,970	91	29	8.5	19	12.3	3,187
ARKANSAS	12,219	74	48	7.4	20	14.3	2,359
CALIFORNIA	18,753	114	9	8.1	17.8	10.5	26,365
COLORADO	16,463	100	20	8.3	18.5	8.8	3,231
CONNECTICUT	23,059	140	1	6.4	17.4	13	3,174
DELAWARE	17,661	107	10	7.1	18.1	11.2	622
D. OF COLUMBIA	21,389	130	3	7	14	12.1	626
FLORIDA	16,603	101	17	6.6	15.7	17.6	11,366
GEORGIA	15,260	93	27	7.6	20.1	9.9	5,976
HAWAII	16,753	102	15	8.8	18.7	9.4	1,054
IDAHO	12,665	77	45	9.4	22.8	10.9	1,005
ILLINOIS	17,575	107	12	7.7	19.2	11.9	11,535
INDIANA	14,924	91	30	7.3	20.1	11.7	5,499
IOWA	14,662	89	33	7.5	19.3	14.3	2,884
KANSAS	15,759	96	22	8.3	18.9	13.3	2,450
KENTUCKY	12,822	78	43	7.3	20.1	11.9	3,726
LOUISIANA	12,292	75	47	9.1	21.2	9.8	4,481
MAINE	15,106	92	28	7.1	19	13.2	1,164
MARYLAND	19,487	118	5	7.1	17.9	10.4	4,392
MASSACHUSETTS	20,816	126	4	6.5	17	13.4	5,822
MICHIGAN	16,552	100	18	7.2	20.1	11.2	9,088
MINNESOTA	16,674	101	16	8	19.2	12.5	4,193
MISSISSIPPI	11,116	67	51	8.4	21.8	11.9	2,613
MISSOURI	15,452	94	25	7.5	18.9	13.7	5,029
MONTANA	12,866	78	40	8.5	19.9	11.8	826
NEBRASKA	14,774	90	32	8.3	19.6	13.5	1,606
NEVADA	17,511	106	13	7.2	16.4	9.9	936
NEW HAMPSHIRE	19,434	118	6	7	18.4	11.6	998
NEW JERSEY	21,994	133	2	6.6	18.1	12.6	7,562
NEW MEXICO	12,488	76	46	9.5	21.4	9.6	1,450
NEW YORK	19,305	117	7	6.8	17.8	12.7	17,783
NORTH CAROLINA	14,304	87	35	6.7	18.7	11.3	6,255
NORTH DAKOTA	12,833	78	42	8.9	19.9	12.7	685
OHIO	15,536	94	23	7.3	19.4	12.1	10,744
OKLAHOMA	13,323	81	38	8.5	19.6	12.3	3,301
OREGON	14,885	90	31	7.5	18.9	13.2	2,687
PENNSYLVANIA	16,233	98	21	6.6	17.1	14.3	11,853
RHODE ISLAND	16,892	102	14	6.4	16.9	14.4	968
SOUTH CAROLINA	12,926	78	39	7.5	20	10.2	3,347
SOUTH DAKOTA	12,755	77	44	9	20.1	13.7	708
TENNESSEE	13,873	84	36	6.8	19.1	12.1	4,762
TEXAS	14,586	88	34	8.9	20.4	9.4	16,370
UTAH	12,193	74	49	11.8	25.5	7.9	1,645
VERMONT	15,302	93	26	7.4	18.7	11.8	535
VIRGINIA	17,675	107	10	7.1	18.2	10.3	5,706
WASHINGTON	16,473	100	19	7.9	18.9	11.4	4,409
WEST VIRGINIA	11,735	71	50	6.6	20.1	13.3	1,936
WISCONSIN	15,524	94	24	7.6	19.3	12.9	4,775
WYOMING	13,609	83	37	9.9	21.5	8.3	509
UNITED STATES	16,489	100		7.6	18.8	12	238,740

x

Birth Rate 1987 per 1000 population	Death Rate 1987 per 1000 population	Natural increase Birth Rate – Death Rate 1987	Infantile Mortality Deaths - 1 year per 1000 live births 1987	Metropolitan Part of State 1985 %	
14.6	9.2	5.4	12.2	63.6	ALABAMA
22.2	3.9	18.3	10.4	45.3	ALASKA
18.7	8	10.7	9.5	76.3	ARIZONA
14.5	10.2	4.3	10.2	39.1	ARKANSAS
18.2	7.6	10.6	9	95.7	CALIFORNIA
16.3	6.4	9.9	9.8	81.2	COLORADO
14.6	8.8	5.8	8.8	92.6	CONNECTICUT
15.4	8.7	6.7	11.7	66.3	DELAWARE
16.4	11.9	4.5	19.3	100	D. OF COLUMBIA
14.6	10.6	4	10.6	91	FLORIDA
16.5	8.1	8.4	12.7	63.9	GEORGIA
17.2	5.7	11.5	8.9	77.3	HAWAII
16	7.4	8.6	10.4	19.1	IDAHO
15.6	8.8	6.8	11.6	82.3	ILLINOIS
14.2	8.8	5.4	10.1	68	INDIANA
13.4	9.6	3.8	9.1	42.3	IOWA
15.6	8.9	6.7	9.5	50.1	KANSAS
13.8	9.3	4.5	9.7	45.5	KENTUCKY
16.6	8.2	8.4	11.8	69.1	LOUISIANA
14.2	9.5	4.7	8.3	36.1	MAINE
16	8.4	7.6	1.5	92.9	MARYLAND
14.4	9 5	4.9	7.2	90.9	MASSACHUSETTS
15.3	8 7	6.6	10.7	80.2	MICHIGAN
15.3	8.1	7.2	8.7	65.4	MINNESOTA
15.7	9.4	6.3	13.7	29.4	MISSISSIPPI
14.7	9.9	4.8	10.2	65.6	MISSOURI
15.1	8.2	6.9	10	24.3	MONTANA
14.9	9.3	5.6	8.6	46.5	NEBRASKA
16.6	7.8	8.8	9.6	82.7	NEVADA
16.1	8	8.1	7.8	56.2	NEW HAMPSHIRE
14.8	9.4	5.4	9.4	100	NEW JERSEY
18.2	6.9	11.3	8.1	47.3	NEW MEXICO
15.3	9.7	5.6	10.7	90.5	NEW YORK
14.6	8.6	6	11.9	54.9	NORTH CAROLINA
15.3	8.2	7.1	8.7	36.4	NORTH DAKOTA
14.6	9.2	5.4	9.3	78.8	OHIO
14.6	9	5.6	9.6	58.3	OKLAHOMA
14.2	8.9	5.3	10.4	67.2	OREGON
13.6	10.5	3.1	10.4	84.6	PENNSYLVANIA
14.2	9.8	4.4	8.4	92.5	RHODE ISLAND
15.4	8.3	7.1	12.7	60	SOUTH CAROLINA
16.2	9.4	6.8	9.9	27.9	SOUTH DAKOTA
14	9.3	4.7	11.7	66.6	TENNESSEE
18	7.1	10.9	9.1	80.5	TEXAS
21	5.4	15.6	10.5	76.8	UTAH
14.8	8.7	6.1	8.5	22.8	VERMONT
15.3	7.9	7.4	10.2	71.3	VIRGINIA
15.5	7.7	7.8	9.7	80.9	WASHINGTON
11.8	10.4	1.4	9.8	36.7	WEST VIRGINIA
14.8	8.8	6	8.6	66.5	WISCONSIN
15.4	6.2	9.2	9.2	28.6	WYOMING
15.7	8.7	7	10.1	76.5	UNITED STATES

UNITED STATES – CITIES

	Population 1990	Rank	Density Persons per square mile	Population Change 1980-1990 %	Population 1980
AKRON	223,019	71	3,705	-6.0	237,177
ALBUQUERQUE	384,736	38	3,543	15.6	332,920
ANAHEIM	266,406	59	6,181	21.4	219,494
ANCHORAGE	226,338	69	131	29.8	174,431
ARLINGTON	261,721	61	3,180	63.5	160,113
ATLANTA	394,017	36	3,003	-7.3	425,022
AURORA	222,103	72	3,537	40.1	158,588
AUSTIN	465,622	27	3,369	34.6	345,890
BAKERSFIELD	174,820	97	2,288	65.5	105,611
BALTIMORE	736,014	13	9,166	-6.4	786,741
BATON ROUGE	219,531	73	3,011	-0.4	220,394
BIRMINGHAM	265,968	60	2,665	-6.5	284,413
BOSTON	574,283	20	12,167	2.0	562,994
BUFFALO	328,123	50	7,850	-8.3	357,870
CHARLOTTE	395,934	35	2,615	25.5	315,474
CHICAGO	2,783,726	3	12,204	-7.4	3,005,072
CINCINNATI	364,040	45	4,667	-5.5	385,409
CLEVELAND	505,616	24	6,400	-11.9	573,822
COLORADO SPRINGS	281,140	54	2,072	30.7	215,105
COLUMBUS, GA	179,278	93	824	5.4	170,108
COLUMBUS,OH	632,910	16	3,406	12.0	565,021
CORPUS CHRISTI	257,453	64	1,526	10.9	232,134
DALLAS	1,006,877	8	3,038	11.3	904,599
DAYTON	182,044	89	3,346	-5.9	193,536
DENVER	467,610	26	4,378	-5.1	492,686
DES MOINES	193,187	80	2,923	1.1	191,003
DETROIT	1,027,974	7	7,581	-14.6	1,203,368
EL PASO	515,342	22	2,150	21.2	425,259
FORT WAYNE	173,072	99	3,000	0.4	172,391
FORT WORTH	447,619	28	1,746	16.2	385,164
FREMONT	173,339	98	2,211	31.4	131,945
FRESNO	354,202	47	3,805	62.9	217,491
GARLAND	180,650	91	3,220	30.1	138,857
GLENDALE	180,038	92	5,884	29.5	139,060
GRAND RAPIDS	189,126	83	4,358	4.0	181,843
GREENSBORO	183,521	88	2,592	17.9	155,642
HIALEAH	188,004	85	9,691	29.4	145,254
HONOLULU	365,272	44	4,199	0.1	365,048
HOUSTON	1,630,553	4	2,885	2.2	1,595,138
HUNTINGTON BEACH	181,519	90	6,673	6.5	170,505
INDIANAPOLIS	741,952	12	2,108	4.3	711,539
JACKSON	196,637	78	1,852	-3.1	202,895
JACKSONVILLE	672,971	15	886	17.9	571,003
JERSEY CITY	228,537	67	17,313	2.2	223,532
KANSAS CITY	435,146	31	1,376	-2.9	448,028
LAS VEGAS	258,295	63	3,849	56.9	164,674
LEXINGTON-FAYETTE	225,366	70	792	10.4	204,165
LINCOLN	191,972	81	3,152	11.7	171,932
LITTLE ROCK	175,795	96	2,088	10.5	159,159
LONG BEACH	429,433	32	8,623	18.8	361,498

Rank 1980	Change in Rank 1980-1990	Black % 1980	Spanish % 1980	- 18 Years 1980	+ 65 Years 1980	
59	-12	22.2	0.6	26.4	13.5	AKRON
44	6	2.5	33.8	27.8	8.4	ALBUQUERQUE
63	4	1.2	17.2	26.5	7.7	ANAHEIM
78	9	5.3	3	31.5	2	ANCHORAGE
94	33	2.9	4.1	28.5	4.5	ARLINGTON
29	-7	66.6	1.4	26.8	11.5	ATLANTA
97	25	6.9	5	29.5	4.3	AURORA
42	15	12.2	18.7	24.5	7.5	AUSTIN
152	55	10.6	15	29.1	9.2	BAKERSFIELD
10	-3	54.8	1	26.9	12.8	BALTIMORE
62	-11	36.5	1.8	27.3	8.7	BATON ROUGE
50	-10	55.6	0.8	26.6	13.9	BIRMINGHAM
21	1	22.4	6.4	21.6	12.7	BOSTON
39	-11	26.6	2.7	25.2	15	BUFFALO
47	12	31	1.1	27.8	8.6	CHARLOTTE
2	-1	39.8	14	28.4	11.4	CHICAGO
32	-13	33.8	0.8	25.2	14.5	CINCINNATI
18	-6	43.8	3.1	27.8	13	CLEVELAND
66	12	5.6	8.5	28.3	8.3	COLORADO SPRINGS
86	-7	34.2	2.1	29.5	8.9	COLUMBUS, GA
20	4	22.1	0.8	25.8	8.9	COLUMBUS,OH
60	-4	5.1	46.6	32.4	8.2	CORPUS CHRISTI
7	-1	29.4	12.3	27	9.5	DALLAS
73	-16	36.9	0.9	27.4	11.8	DAYTON
24	-2	12	18.8	22.5	12.6	DENVER
74	-6	6.8	1.8	25.9	12.5	DES MOINES
6	-1	63.1	2.4	30.3	11.7	DETROIT
28	6	3.2	62.5	35	6.9	EL PASO
80	-19	14.6	2.2	28	11.9	FORT WAYNE
33	5	22.8	12.6	27.1	11.8	FORT WORTH
119	21	2.5	14	30.1	5.2	FREMONT
65	18	9.5	23.6	27.9	10.9	FRESNO
115	24	5.3	6.3	33.7	4.1	GARLAND
114	22	0.3	17.8	20.8	16.3	GLENDALE
75	-8	15.7	3.2	27.4	13.4	GRAND RAPIDS
100	12	33	0.8	25.3	9.8	GREENSBORO
108	23	1.5	74.3	24.2	11.4	HIALEAH
36	-8	1.2	5.2	23.1	10.4	HONOLULU
5	1	27.6	17.6	28.4	6.9	HOUSTON
85	-5	0.7	7.9	27.9	5.9	HUNTINGTON BEACH
12	0	21.8	0.9	28.6	10.3	INDIANAPOLIS
70	-8	47	0.7	29.6	9.7	JACKSON
19	4	25.4	1.8	28.8	9.6	JACKSONVILLE
61	-6	27.7	18.6	29.4	11.8	JERSEY CITY
27	-4	27.4	3.3	26.5	12.3	KANSAS CITY
89	26	12.8	7.8	27.9	8.3	LAS VEGAS
68	-2	13.3	0.7	25.3	8.6	LEXINGTON-FAYETTE
81	0	2	1.6	23.5	10.3	LINCOLN
96	0	32.2	0.8	28	11	LITTLE ROCK
37	5	11.3	14	22.9	14	LONG BEACH

UNITED STATES – CITIES

	Population 1990	Rank	Density Persons per square mile	Population Change 1980-1990 %	Population 1980
LOS ANGELES	3,485,398	2	7,481	17.4	2,368,528
LOUISVILLE	269,063	58	4,404	-9.9	298,694
LUBBOCK	186,206	87	1,849	6.8	174,361
MADISON	191,262	82	3,440	12.1	170,616
MEMPHIS	610,337	18	2,247	-5.5	646,174
MESA	288,091	53	3,438	89.0	152,404
MIAMI	358,548	46	10,453	3.4	346,681
MILWAUKEE	628,088	17	6,556	-1.3	636,297
MINNEAPOLIS	368,383	42	6,686	-0.7	370,951
MOBILE	196,278	79	1,596	-2.1	200,452
MONTGOMERY	187,106	86	1,458	5.2	177,857
NASHVILLE-DAV.	510,784	23	1,065	6.9	477,811
NEW ORLEANS	496,938	25	2,492	-10.9	557,927
NEW YORK	7,322,564	1	24,287	3.5	7,071,639
NEWARK	275,221	56	11,420	-16.4	329,248
NEWPORT NEWS	170,045	100	2,604	17.4	144,903
NORFOLK	261,229	62	4,929	-2.2	266,979
OAKLAND	372,242	39	6,906	9.7	339,337
OKLAHOMA	444,719	29	736	10.1	404,014
OMAHA	335,795	48	3,458	7.0	313,939
PHILADELPHIA	1,585,577	5	11,659	-6.1	1,688,210
PHOENIX	983,403	9	2,545	24.5	789,704
PITTSBURGH	369,879	40	6,677	-12.8	423,959
PORTLAND	437,319	30	4,012	18.8	368,148
RALEIGH	207,951	75	3,403	38.4	150,255
RICHMOND	203,056	76	3,379	-7.4	219,214
RIVERSIDE	226,505	68	3,103	32.8	170,591
ROCHESTER	231,636	66	6,773	-4.2	241,741
SACRAMENTO	369,365	41	3,804	34.0	275,741
ST. LOUIS	396,685	34	6,461	-12.4	452,801
ST. PAUL	272,235	57	5,195	0.7	270,230
ST. PETERSBURG	238,629	65	4,269	0	238,647
SAN ANTONIO	935,933	10	3,368	19.1	785,940
SAN DIEGO	1,110,549	6	3,448	26.8	875,538
SAN FRANCISCO	723,959	14	15,603	6.6	678,974
SAN JOSE	782,248	11	4,631	24.3	629,400
SANTA ANA	293,742	52	10,721	44.0	204,023
SEATTLE	516,259	21	6,175	4.5	493,846
SHREVEPORT	198,525	77	2,292	-4.1	206,989
SPOKANE	177,196	94	3,187	3.4	171,300
STOCKTON	210,943	74	4,940	42.3	148,283
TACOMA	176,664	95	3,696	11.5	158,501
TAMPA	280,015	55	3,298	3.1	271,577
TOLEDO	332,943	49	3,950	-6.1	354,635
TUCSON	405,390	33	3,248	22.6	330,537
TULSA	367,302	43	1,974	1.8	360,919
VIRGINIA BEACH	393,069	37	1,740	49.9	262,199
WASHINGTON	606,900	19	9,679	-4.9	638,432
WICHITA	304,011	51	2,712	8.6	279,838
YONKERS	188,082	84	10,278	-3.7	195,351

Rank 1980	Change in Rank 1980-1990	Black % 1980	Spanish % 1980	-18 Years 1980	+65 Years 1980	
3	1	17	27.5	25.1	10.6	LOS ANGELES
49	-9	28.2	0.7	25	15.3	LOUISVILLE
79	-8	8.2	18.8	27.7	7.8	LUBBOCK
83	1	2.7	1.3	20.5	8.7	MADISON
14	-4	47.6	0.8	29.1	10.4	MEMPHIS
102	49	1.2	9.1	30.1	11.2	MESA
41	-5	25.1	55.9	21.4	17	MIAMI
16	-1	23.1	4.1	27	12.5	MILWAUKEE
34	-8	7.7	1.3	20	15.4	MINNEAPOLIS
71	-8	36.2	1.1	29	11.1	MOBILE
76	-10	39.2	0.9	30.2	10.1	MONTGOMERY
25	2	23.3	0.8	25	11	NASHVILLE-DAV.
22	-3	55.3	3.4	28.8	11.7	NEW ORLEANS
1	0	25.2	19.9	25	13.5	NEW YORK
46	-10	58.2	18.6	34.1	8.8	NEWARK
109	9	31.5	1.8	28.4	7.8	NEWPORT NEWS
55	-7	35.2	2.3	24.6	9.2	NORFOLK
43	4	46.9	9.6	24.3	13.2	OAKLAND
31	2	14.6	2.8	27	11.3	OKLAHOMA
48	0	12	2.3	27.5	12.2	OMAHA
4	-1	37.8	3.8	25.9	14.1	PHILADELPHIA
9	0	4.8	14.8	29	9.3	PHOENIX
30	-10	24	0.8	21.4	16	PITTSBURGH
35	5	7.6	2.1	21.8	15.3	PORTLAND
105	30	27.4	0.9	22.3	8.3	RALEIGH
64	-12	51.3	1	22.4	14.1	RICHMOND
84	16	6.9	16.2	29.2	8.8	RIVERSIDE
57	-9	25.8	5.4	26.6	14	ROCHESTER
52	11	13.4	14.2	24.6	13.6	SACRAMENTO
26	-8	45.6	1.2	26.1	17.6	ST. LOUIS
54	-3	4.9	2.9	24.1	15	ST. PAUL
58	-7	17.2	1.8	20.4	25.8	ST. PETERSBURG
11	1	7.3	53.7	32.2	9.5	SAN ANTONIO
8	2	8.9	14.9	24.1	9.7	SAN DIEGO
13	-1	12.7	12.3	17.2	15.4	SAN FRANCISCO
17	6	4.6	22.3	31	6.2	SAN JOSE
69	17	4	44.5	30.6	7.4	SANTA ANA
23	2	9.5	2.6	17.6	15.4	SEATTLE
67	-10	41.1	1.3	30.3	11.7	SHREVEPORT
82	-12	1.6	1.5	24.5	15.3	SPOKANE
107	33	10.4	22.1	29.2	11	STOCKTON
98	3	9.2	2.4	26.8	13.5	TACOMA
53	-2	23.5	13.3	25.1	14.8	TAMPA
40	9	17.4	3	28.1	12.5	TOLEDO
45	12	3.7	24.9	25.5	11.7	TUCSON
38	-5	11.8	1.7	25.8	10.8	TULSA
56	19	10	2	30.7	4.5	VIRGINIA BEACH
15	-4	70.3	2.8	22.5	11.6	WASHINGTON
51	0	10.8	3.5	26.3	10.6	WICHITA
72	-12	10.5	8.7	23.1	14.8	YONKERS

UNITED STATES – URBAN AREAS

	Population 1988 (Thousands)	Rank	Population 1970 (Thousands)	Rank	Change in Rank 1970-1988
ALBANY-SCHENECTADY	851	48	811	41	-7
ATLANTA	2,737	13	1,684	18	5
BALTIMORE	2,342	18	2,089	14	-4
BIRMINGHAM	923	46	794	42	-4
BOSTON-LAWRENCE-SALEM	4,110	7	3,939	7	0
BUFFALO-NIAGARA FALLS	1,176	33	1,349	23	-10
CHARLOTTE-GASTONIA-ROCK HILL	1,112	35	840	39	4
CHICAGO-GARY-LAKE COUNTY	8,181	3	7,779	3	0
CINCINNATI-HAMILTON	1,728	23	1,613	19	-4
CLEVELAND-AKRON-LORAIN	2,769	12	3,000	9	-3
COLUMBUS	1,344	29	1,149	25	-4
DALLAS-FORT WORTH	3,766	8	2,352	12	4
DAYTON-SPRINGFIELD	948	44	975	33	-11
DENVER-BOULDER	1,858	22	1,238	24	2
DETROIT-ANN ARBOR	4,620	6	4,788	5	-1
GREENSBORO-WINSTON-SALEM-HIGH PT.	925	45	743	43	-2
HARTFORD-NEW. BR.-MIDDLET.-BRIS.	1,108	36	1,000	32	-4
HONOLULU	838	50	631	48	-2
HOUSTON-GALVESTON-BRAZORIA	3,641	10	2,169	13	3
INDIANAPOLIS	1,237	32	1,111	26	-6
JACKSONVILLE	898	47	613	49	2
KANSAS CITY	1,575	24	1,373	21	-3
LOS ANGELES-ANAHEIM-RIVERSIDE	13,770	2	9,981	2	0
LOUISVILLE	967	42	907	36	-6
MEMPHIS	979	39	834	40	1
MIAMI-FORT LAUDERDALE	3,001	11	1,888	16	5
MILWAUKEE-RACINE	1,572	25	1,575	20	-5
MINNEAPOLIS-ST. PAUL	2,388	16	1,982	15	-1
NASHVILLE-DAVIDSON	972	40	699	45	5
NEW ORLEANS	1,307	31	1,100	28	-3
NEW YORK-N.NEW JERSEY-LONG I.	18,120	1	18,193	1	0
NORFOLK-VIRGINIA B.-NEWPORT NEWS	1,380	28	1,059	30	2
OKLAHOMA CITY	964	43	719	44	1
ORLANDO	971	41	453	58	17
PHILADELPHIA-WILMINGTON-TRENTON	5,963	5	5,749	4	-1
PHOENIX	2,030	20	971	34	14
PITTSBURGH-BEAVER VALLEY	2,284	19	2,556	10	-9
PORTLAND-VANCOUVER	1,414	26	1,047	31	5
PROVIDENCE-PAWTUCKET-FALL RIVER	1,125	34	1,065	29	-5
RICHMOND-PETERSBURG	844	49	676	47	-2
ROCHESTER	980	38	962	35	-3
SACRAMENTO	1,385	27	848	38	11
ST. LOUIS	2,467	14	2,429	11	-3
SALT LAKE CITY-OGDEN	1,065	37	684	46	9
SAN ANTONIO	1,323	30	888	37	7
SAN DIEGO	2,370	17	1,358	22	5
SAN FRANCISCO-OAKLAND-SAN JOSE	6,042	4	4,754	6	2
SEATTLE-TACOMA	2,421	15	1,837	17	2
TAMPA-ST. PETERSBURG-CLEARWATER	1,995	21	1,106	27	6
WASHINGTON	3,734	9	3,040	8	-1

These urban areas are the largest Standard Metropolitan Statistical Areas which are defined by the Census Bureau as large centers of population together with adjoining regions that are socially and economically linked to one another.

Population Change 1970-1988 %	Rank	Black % 1980	Spanish % 1980	-18 Years 1980	+65 Years 1980	Population 1980 (Thousands)
5	39	4	1	27	13	836
63	7	25	1	29	8	2, 138
12	32	26	1	27	10	2, 200
16	30	27	1	28	12	884
4	40	4	2	26	12	3, 972
-13	50	9	1	27	12	1, 243
32	19	20	1	29	10	971
5	38	20	8	29	10	7, 937
7	35	11	1	29	11	1, 660
-8	48	15	2	28	11	2, 834
17	29	11	1	28	9	1, 244
60	8	14	9	29	8	2, 931
-3	46	13	1	29	10	942
50	11	5	11	28	8	1, 618
-4	47	19	2	29	9	4,753
24	24	19	1	27	10	852
11	34	7	4	26	11	1, 014
33	18	2	7	28	7	763
68	5	18	15	31	6	3, 101
11	33	14	1	30	10	1, 167
46	13	22	2	29	10	722
15	31	13	2	28	11	1 , 433
38	15	9	24	28	10	11,498
7	36	13	1	29	10	957
17	28	40	1	31	9	913
59	9	15	24	23	18	2, 644
0	44	11	3	29	11	1, 570
20	26	2	1	28	10	2, 137
39	14	16	1	28	10	851
19	27	33	4	30	9	1, 256
0	45	16	12	26	12	17, 539
30	21	28	2	29	8	1, 160
34	17	9	2	28	10	861
114	1	13	4	27	11	700
4	41	18	3	27	12	5, 681
109	2	3	13	28	12	1, 509
-11	49	8	1	25	13	2, 423
35	16	3	2	27	11	1, 298
6	37	2	2	26	13	1, 083
25	23	29	1	27	10	761
2	42	8	2	28	11	971
63	6	6	10	27	10	1, 100
2	43	17	1	29	12	2, 377
56	10	1	5	36	7	910
49	12	7	45	32	9	1,072
75	4	6	15	26	10	1, 862
27	22	9	12	25	10	5,368
32	20	4	2	26	1 0	2, 093
80	3	9	5	22	22	1, 614
23	25	27	3	27	8	3, 251

TIME ZONES

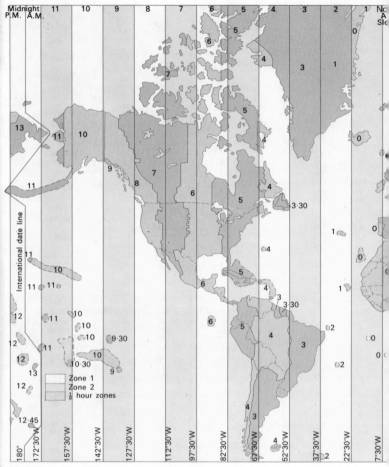

WORLD TIMES AT 12.00 G.M.T.

Time zones

The world is divided into 24 time zones, each centred on meridians at 15° intervals which is the longitudinal distance the sun appears to travel every hour. The meridian running through Greenwich passes through the middle of the first zone. Successive zones to the east of Greenwich zone are ahead of Greenwich time by one hour for every 15° of longitude, while zones to the west are behind by one hour.

The International Date Line

When it is 12 noon at the Greenwich meridian, 180° east it is midnight of the same day while 180° west the day is only just beginning. To overcome this the International Date Line was established, approximately following the 180° meridian. Thus, for example, if one travelled eastwards from Japan (140° East) to Samoa (170° West) one would pass from Sunday night into Sunday morning.

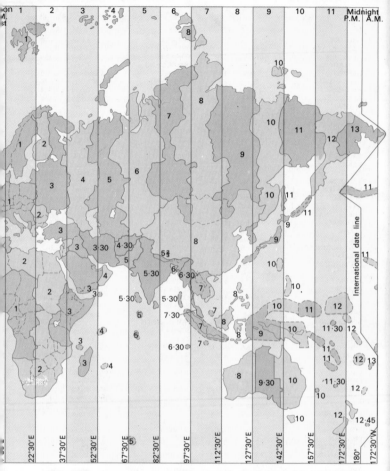

This table shows the time difference from Greenwich Mean Time for a selection of world cities.

During the summer months Daylight Saving schemes operate in some countries and affect the times by an hour.

City	GMT	City	GMT
Anchorage	−10	Paris	+1
Chicago	−6	Peking	+8
Delhi	+5.30	Rio de Janeiro	−3
Johannesburg	+2	Stockholm	+1
Lagos	+1	Sydney	+10
Los Angeles	−8	Tehran	+3.30
Mexico	−6	Tokyo	+9
Moscow	+3	Toronto	−5
New York	−5	Washington	−5

WORLD CITIES

City	Country	Population (Thousands)
ABIDJAN	Ivory Coast	1,850
ADDIS ABABA	Ethiopia	1,686
ADELAIDE	Australia	1,013
AHMADABAD	India	2,548
ALEPPO	Syria	1,191
ALEXANDRIA	Egypt	2,893
ALGIERS	Algeria	1,722
ALMA-ATA	USSR	1,108
AMMAN	Jordan	1,160
AMSTERDAM	Netherlands	1,038
ANKARA	Turkey	2,252
ANSHAN	China	1,298
ATHENS	Greece	3,027
ATLANTA	USA	2,737
BAGHDAD	Iraq	4,649
BAKU	USSR	1,757
BALTIMORE	USA	2,342
BANDUNG	Indonesia	1,462
BANGALORE	India	2,922
BANGKOK	Thailand	5,609
BAOTOU	China	1,119
BARCELONA	Spain	1,704
BEIJING *	China	9,750
BELEM	Brazil	1,296
BELGRADE	Yugoslavia	1,470
BELO HORIZONTE	Brazil	3,446
BERLIN	Germany	3,301
BIRMINGHAM	UK	1,007
BOGOTÁ	Colombia	4,185
BOMBAY *	India	8,243
BOSTON	USA	4,110
BOZHOU	China	1,112
BRASILIA	Brazil	1,557
BRISBANE	Australia	1,215
BUCHAREST	Romania	1,976
BUDAPEST	Hungary	2,115
BUENOS AIRES *	Argentina	10,728
BUFFALO	USA	1,176
CAIRO *	Egypt	6,325
CALCUTTA *	India	9,194
CALI	Colombia	1,397
CANTON	China	3,359
CAPE TOWN	South Africa	1,912
CARACAS	Venezuela	3,247
CASABLANCA	Morocco	2,158
CHANGCHUN	China	1,908
CHANGSHA	China	1,193
CHANGSHU	China	1,004
CHAO'AN	China	1,227
CHARLOTTE	USA	1,112
CHELYABINSK	USSR	1,179
CHENGDU	China	2,642
CHICAGO *	USA	8,181
CHITTAGONG	Bangladesh	1,840
CHONGQING	China	2,832
CINCINNATI	USA	1,728
CLEVELAND	USA	2,769
COLOMBO	Sri Lanka	1,412
COLUMBUS	USA	1,344
COPENHAGEN	Denmark	1,339
CORDOBA	Argentina	1,055
CURITIBA	Brazil	1,926
DACCA	Bangladesh	4,770
DAKAR	Senegal	1,382
DALIAN	China	1,682
DALLAS	USA	3,766
DAMASCUS	Syria	1,219
DAR ES SALAAM	Tanzania	1,096
DATONG	China	1,020
DELHI	India	5,729
DENVER	USA	1,858
DETROIT	USA	4,620
DNEPROPETROVSK	USSR	1,179
DONETSK	USSR	1,110
DONGGUANG	China	1,230
DOUALA	Cameroon	1,030
EAST RAND	South Africa	1,038
EL GIZA	Egypt	1,858
FAISALABAD	Pakistan	1,104
FORTALEZA	Brazil	2,169
FUKUOKA	Japan	1,160
FUSHUN	China	1,270
FUZHOU	China	1,205
GORKI	USSR	1,438
GUADALAJARA	Mexico	2,587
GUATEMALA	Guatemala	2,000
GUAYAQUIL	Ecuador	1,301
GUIYANG	China	1,403
HAIPHONG	Vietnam	1,279
HAMBURG	Germany	1,594
HANDAN	China	1,014
HANGZHOU	China	1,271
HANOI	Vietnam	2,571
HARBIN	China	2,668
HARTFORD	USA	1,108
HAVANA	Cuba	2,059
HEZE	China	1,017
HIROSHIMA	Japan	1,044
HO CHI MINH	Vietnam	3,420
HONG KONG	Hong Kong	1,176
HOUSTON	USA	3,641
HUAINAN	China	1,019
HYDERABAD	India	2,546
IBADAN	Nigeria	1,060
INCHON	Korea, S.	1,387
INDIANAPOLIS	USA	1,237
ISTANBUL	Turkey	5,495
IZMIR	Turkey	1,490
JAIPUR	India	1,015
JAKARTA *	Indonesia	7,3480
JEDDA	Saudi Arabia	1,400
JILIN	China	1,169
JINAN	China	1,464
JOHANNESBURG	South Africa	1,762
KABUL	Afghanistan	1,127
KANPUR	India	1,639
KANSAS CITY	USA	1,575
KAOHSIUNG	Taiwan	1,300
KARACHI	Pakistan	5,181
KAWASAKI	Japan	1,089
KAZAN	USSR	1,094
KHARKHOV	USSR	1,611
KIEV	USSR	2,587
KINSHASA	Zaïre	2,654
KITAKYUSHU	Japan	1,056
KOBE	Japan	1,411
KOWLOON	Hong Kong	2,302
KUALA LUMPUR	Malaysia	1,103
KUNMING	China	1,516
KWANGJU	Korea, S.	1,165
KYOTO	Japan	1,479
KYUBYSHEV	USSR	1,257
LAGOS	Nigeria	1,097
LAHORE	Pakistan	2,953
LAIWU	China	1,054
LANZHOU	China	1,391
LENINGRAD	USSR	5,020
LESHAN	China	1,039
LIMA-CALLAO	Peru	4,605
LINHAI	China	1,012
LINYI	China	1,385
LISBON	Portugal	1,612

City	Country	Population (Thousands)	City	Country	Population (Thousands)
LONDON *	UK	6,735	RANGOON	Burma	2,459
LOS ANGELES *	USA	13,770	RECIFE	Brazil	2,945
LUANDA	Angola	1,200	RIO DE JANEIRO *	Brazil	11,141
LUCKNOW	India	1,008	RIYADH	Saudi Arabia	2,000
LUOYANG	China	1,063	ROME	Italy	2,817
LUPANSHUI	China	2,247	ROSARIO	Argentina	1,016
LYONS	France	1,170	ROSTOV	USSR	1,020
MACHENG	China	1,010	ROTTERDAM	Netherlands	1,040
MADRAS	India	4,289	SACRAMENTO	USA	1,385
MADRID	Spain	3,101	SAINT LOUIS	USA	2,467
MANILA	Philippines	1,728	SALT LAKE CITY	USA	1,065
MAPUTO	Mozambique	1,070	SALVADOR	Brazil	2,362
MARACAIBO	Venezuela	1,295	SAN ANTONIO	USA	1,323
MARSEILLES	France	1,080	SAN DIEGO	USA	2,370
MASSHAD	Iran	1,464	SAN FRANCISCO *	USA	6,042
MEDAN	Indonesia	1,379	SAN JUAN	Puerto Rico	1,816
MEDELLIN	Colombia	1,506	SANTIAGO	Chile	4,858
MELBOURNE	Australia	2,965	SANTO DOMINGO	Dominican Rep	1,313
MEXICO CITY *	Mexico	18,748	SÃO PAULO *	Brazil	16,832
MIAMI	USA	3,001	SAPPORO	Japan	1,543
MILAN	Italy	1,464	SEATTLE	USA	2,421
MILWAUKEE	USA	1,572	SEMARANG	Indonesia	1,026
MINNEAPOLIS-SP.	USA	2,388	SEOUL *	Korea, S.	10,513
MINSK	USSR	1,589	SHANGHAI *	China	12,320
MOGADISHU	Somali Rep.	1,000	SHENYANG	China	4,285
MONTEVIDEO	Uruguay	1,248	SHIJIAZHUANG	China	1,187
MONTREAL	Canada	2,921	SINGAPORE	Singapore	2,600
MONTERREY	Mexico	2,335	SOFIA	Bulgaria	1,129
MOSCOW *	USSR	8,967	STOCKHOLM	Sweden	1,471
MUNICH	Germany	1,189	SUINING	China	1,195
NAGOYA	Japan	2,116	SURABAJA	Indonesia	2,028
NAGPUR	India	1,302	SVERDLOVSK	USSR	1,367
NAIROBI	Kenya	1,200	SYDNEY	Australia	3,531
NANCHANG	China	2,289	TAEGU	Korea, S.	2,031
NANJING	China	2,290	TAIPEI	Taiwan	2,680
NAPLES	Italy	1,203	TAIYUAN	China	1,929
NEW ORLEANS	USA	1,307	TAMPA	USA	1,995
NEW YORK *	USA	18,120	TANGSHAN	China	1,410
NINGBO	China	1,033	TASHKENT	USSR	2,073
NORFOLK	USA	1,380	TBILISI	USSR	1,194
NOVA IGUAÇU	Brazil	1,325	TEHRAN *	Iran	6,043
NOVOSIBIRSK	USSR	1,436	TIANJIN	China	5,459
ODESSA	USSR	1,115	TOKYO *	Japan	11,829
OMSK	USSR	1,148	TORONTO	Canada	3,427
OPORTO	Portugal	1,315	TURIN	Italy	1,012
OSAKA	Japan	2,636	UFA	USSR	1,083
PARIS *	France	8,510	URUMCHI	China	1,038
PERM	USSR	1,091	VALENCIA	Venezuela	1,135
PERTH	Australia	1,083	VANCOUVER	Canada	1,381
PHILADELPHIA	USA	5,963	VIENNA	Austria	1,531
PHOENIX	USA	2,030	WARSAW	Poland	1,671
PINGXIANG	China	1,305	WASHINGTON	USA	3,734
PITTSBURGH	USA	2,284	WUHAN	China	3,493
POONA	India	1,686	XI'AN	China	2,387
PORT-AU-PRINCE	Haiti	1,144	XIAOGAN	China	1,219
PORTLAND	USA	1,414	XINTAI	China	1,167
PÔRTO ALEGRE	Brazil	2,924	XINTAO	China	1,272
PRAGUE	Czechoslovakia	1,211	YANGCHENG	China	1,265
PROVIDENCE	USA	1,125	YEREVAN	USSR	1,199
PUEBLA	Mexico	1,218	YOKOHAMA	Japan	2,993
PUSAN	Korea, S.	3,517	YULIN	China	1,255
PUYANG	China	1,125	ZAGREB	Yugoslavia	1,175
PYONGYANG	Korea, N.	2,639	ZHAOZHUANG	China	1,612
QINGDAO	China	1,273	ZHENGZHOU	China	1,610
QIQIHAR	China	1,301	ZIBO	China	2,329
QUEZON CITY	Philippines	1,326	ZHONGSHAN	China	1,073
QUITO	Ecuador	1,110			

This list shows the cities of the world that have over 1,000,000 inhabitants. The asterisk indicates the twenty largest. The figures are the latest available and are for the built-up area of a city which is often a larger and more populated area than that of the city within its legal boundaries.

WORLD COUNTRIES

Country	Area (Thousand Square Miles)	Population (Thousands)	Density of Population (Per Square Mile)	Annual Income $	Capital City
AFGHANISTAN	252	15,814	63	450	KABUL
ALBANIA	11	3,202	303	800	TIRANA
ALGERIA	920	24,597	27	2,170	ALGIERS
ANGOLA	481	9,747	20	620	LUANDA
ARGENTINA	1,068	31,929	30	2,160	BUENOS AIRES
AUSTRALIA	2,966	16,807	5.7	14,440	CANBERRA
AUSTRIA	32	7,618	238	17,360	VIENNA
BAHAMAS	5.4	249	64	11,370	NASSAU
BAHRAIN	0.26	489	1,863	7,000	MANAMA
BANGLADESH	56	106,507	2,060	180	DACCA
BARBADOS	0.17	256	1,542	6,370	BRIDGETOWN
BELGIUM	12	9,931	851	16,390	BRUSSELS
BELIZE	8.9	178	20	1,600	BELMOPAN
BENIN	43	4,591	107	380	PORTO-NOVO
BERMUDA	0.02	58	3,004	25,000	HAMILTON
BHUTAN	18	1,483	82	190	THIMPHU
BOLIVIA	424	7,193	17	600	SUCRE
BOTSWANA	225	1,256	5.7	960	GABORONE
BRAZIL	3,286	147,404	45	2,550	BRASILIA
BRUNEI	2.2	249	122	6,000	BANDAR SERI BEGAWAN
BULGARIA	43	9,903	232	2,320	SOFIA
BURKINA FASO	106	8,763	83	310	OUAGADOUGOU
BURMA	261	40,810	161	500	RANGOON
BURUNDI	11	5,302	535	220	BUJUMBURA
CAMBODIA	70	8,055	118	450	PHNOM PENH
CAMEROON	184	11,540	64	1,010	YAOUNDÉ
CANADA	3,852	26,248	7.4	19,020	OTTAWA
CAPE VERDE IS.	1.6	368	237	760	PRAIA
CENT. AFRICAN REP.	241	2,841	12	390	BANGUI
CHAD	496	5,538	11	190	NDJAMENA
CHILE	292	12,961	45	1,770	SANTIAGO
CHINA	3,682	1,119,691	311	360	PEKING
COLOMBIA	440	31,192	78	1,190	BOGOTA
CONGO	132	1,940	15	930	BRAZZAVILLE
COSTA RICA	20	2,922	148	1,790	SAN JOSÉ
CUBA	43	10,594	248	2,000	HAVANA
CYPRUS	3.6	694	195	7,050	NICOSIA
CZECHOSLOVAKIA	49	15,639	323	4,000	PRAGUE
DENMARK	17	5,135	314	20,510	COPENHAGEN
DJIBOUTI	9.0	394	44	1,000	DJIBOUTI
DOMINICA	0.29	80	276	1,800	ROSEAU
DOMINICAN REP.	19	7,018	376	790	SANTO DOMINGO
ECUADOR	109	10,490	98	1,040	QUITO
EGYPT	387	53,080	138	630	CAIRO
EL SALVADOR	8.1	5,207	651	1,040	SAN SALVADOR
EQUATORIAL GUINEA	11	341	31	430	MALABO
ETHIOPIA	472	50,774	119	120	ADDIS ABABA
FIJI	7.1	738	105	1,640	SUVA
FINLAND	131	4,962	42	22,060	HELSINKI
FRANCE	213	56,160	264	17,830	PARIS
FRENCH GUIANA	35	90	2.6	2,000	CAYENNE

This list shows the principal countries of the world with their populations, area and density of population. The latter is calculated from the area of the country less any water area. The area shown in the table is the total area, including such water. The average annual income of each person is shown. This is the total income of the country (the Gross National Product) divided by the population.

Country	Area (Thousand Square Miles)	Population (Thousands)	Density of Population (Per Square Mile)	Annual Income $	Capital City
GABON	103	1,132	11	2,770	LIBREVILLE
GAMBIA, THE	4.4	835	216	230	BANJUL
GERMANY	138	78,620	583	16,500	BERLIN
GHANA	92	14,566	164	380	ACCRA
GIBRALTAR	0.003	31	12,352	4,000	
GREECE	51	10,031	199	5,340	ATHENS
GREENLAND	840	56	0.4	6,000	GODTHAAB
GRENADA	0.13	101	769	1,900	ST. GEORGE'S
GUADELOUPE	0.66	339	520	6,000	BASSE-TERRE
GUATEMALA	42	8,935	213	920	GUATEMALA CITY
GUINEA	95	6,705	71	430	CONAKRY
GUINEA-BISSAU	14	966	89	180	BISSAU
GUYANA	83	1,023	13	310	GEORGETOWN
HAITI	11	5,609	527	400	PORT-AU-PRINCE
HONDURAS	43	4,951	115	900	TEGUCIGALPA
HONG KONG	0.40	5,768	15,090	10,320	
HUNGARY	36	10,563	296	2,560	BUDAPEST
ICELAND	40	251	6.5	21,240	REYKJAVIK
INDIA	1,223	811,817	707	350	DELHI
INDONESIA	735	179,136	256	490	JAKARTA
IRAN	636	55,208	87	4,000	TEHRAN
IRAQ	169	18,279	108	2,000	BAGHDAD
IRELAND	27	3,515	132	8,500	DUBLIN
ISRAEL	10.4	4,566	582	9,750	JERUSALEM
ITALY	116	57,517	507	15,150	ROME
IVORY COAST	125	12,097	99	790	YAMOUSSOUKRO
JAMAICA	4.2	2,375	568	1,260	KINGSTON
JAPAN	146	123,116	847	23,730	TOKYO
JORDAN	34	4,102	119	1,730	AMMAN
KENYA	224	24,872	114	380	NAIROBI
KOREA, NORTH	47	22,418	482	2,000	PYONGYANG
KOREA, SOUTH	38	42,654	1,119	4,400	SEOUL
KUWAIT	6.9	2,048	298	16,380	KUWAIT CITY
LAOS	91	3,972	45	170	VIENTIANE
LEBANON	4.0	2,897	733	2,000	BEIRUT
LESOTHO	12	1,700	145	470	MASERU
LIBERIA	43	2,508	67	500	MONROVIA
LIBYA	679	4,385	6.5	6,000	TRIPOLI
LUXEMBOURG	1.0	378	378	24,860	LUXEMBOURG
MACAU	0.008	448	58,016	2,000	
MADAGASCAR	227	11,602	52	230	ANTANANARIVO
MALAWI	46	8,022	221	180	LILONGWE
MALAYSIA	127	16,957	134	2,130	KUALA LUMPUR
MALI	479	7,960	17	260	BAMAKO
MALTA	0.12	350	2,833	5,820	VALLETTA
MAURITANIA	396	1,969	5.0	490	NOUAKCHOTT
MAURITIUS	0.72	1,068	1,495	1,950	PORT LOUIS
MEXICO	756	84,275	114	1,990	MEXICO CITY
MONACO	0.001	28	38,168	20,000	
MONGOLIA	604	2,158	3.6	400	ULAN BATOR
MOROCCO	172	24,521	142	900	RABAT

Country	Area (Thousand Square Miles)	Population (Thousands)	Density of Population (Per Square Mile)	Annual Income $	Capital City
MOZAMBIQUE	309	15,326	51	80	MAPUTO
NAMIBIA	318	1,817	5.7	1,300	WINDHOEK
NEPAL	54	18,442	349	170	KATMANDU
NETHERLANDS	14	14,891	1,137	16,010	AMSTERDAM
NEW ZEALAND	104	3,389	33	11,800	WELLINGTON
NICARAGUA	50	3,745	82	1,000	MANAGUA
NIGER	489	6,894	14	290	NIAMEY
NIGERIA	357	109,175	310	250	LAGOS (ABUJA)
NORWAY	125	4,227	36	21,850	OSLO
OMAN	82	1,422	17	5,220	MUSCAT
PAKISTAN	307	108,678	365	370	ISLAMABAD
PANAMA	30	2,370	81	1,780	PANAMA CITY
PAPUA NEW GUINEA	179	3,593	21	900	PORT MORESBY
PARAGUAY	157	4,157	27	1,030	ASUNCION
PERU	496	21,792	44	1,090	LIMA
PHILIPPINES	116	60,097	522	700	MANILA
POLAND	121	37,854	322	1,760	WARSAW
PORTUGAL	36	10,467	295	4,260	LISBON
PUERTO RICO	3.4	3,658	1,069	6,010	SAN JUAN
QATAR	4.2	422	99	10,000	DOHA
ROMANIA	92	23,512	264	2,000	BUCHAREST
RWANDA	10	6,989	726	310	KIGALI
SAMOA	1.1	168	154	720	APIA
SAUDI ARABIA	830	14,435	17	6,230	RIYADH
SENEGAL	76	7,171	96	650	DAKAR
SIERRA LEONE	28	4,046	146	200	FREETOWN
SINGAPORE	0.24	2,685	11,400	10,450	SINGAPORE
SOLOMON IS.	11	317	29	570	HONIARA
SOMALIA	246	7,339	30	170	MOGADISHU
SOUTH AFRICA	471	34,492	73	2,460	PRETORIA
SPAIN	195	39,248	204	9,150	MADRID
SRI LANKA	25	16,806	672	430	COLOMBO
SUDAN	967	24,484	27	480	KHARTOUM
SWAZILAND	6.7	763	115	900	MBABANE
SWEDEN	174	8,541	54	21,710	STOCKHOLM
SWITZERLAND	16	6,647	433	30,270	BERN
SYRIA	71	11,719	165	1,020	DAMASCUS
TAIWAN	14	19,950	1,435	6,600	TAIPEI
TANZANIA	365	24,802	72	120	DODOMA
THAILAND	198	55,448	281	1,170	BANGKOK
TOGO	22	3,349	159	390	LOMÉ
TRINIDAD & TOB	2.0	1,263	638	3,160	PORT OF SPAIN
TUNISIA	63	7,990	133	1,260	TUNIS
TURKEY	301	56,741	191	1,360	ANKARA
UGANDA	91	17,804	231	250	KAMPALA
UNITED ARAB EM.	32	1,546	48	18,430	ABU DHABI
UNITED KINGDOM	95	57,205	613	14,570	LONDON
UNITED STATES	3,619	249,928	71	21,100	WASHINGTON
URUGUAY	68	3,077	46	2,620	MONTEVIDEO
USSR	8,649	285,861	33	3,800	MOSCOW
VENEZUELA	352	19,246	57	2,450	CARACAS
VIETNAM	127	65,681	523	450	HANOI
YEMEN	204	10,183	50	640	SANA
YUGOSLAVIA	99	23,764	241	2,490	BELGRADE
ZAIRE	906	34,491	39	260	KINSHASA
ZAMBIA	291	7,804	27	390	LUSAKA
ZIMBABWE	151	9,122	61	640	HARARE

THE WORLD: AIR ROUTES

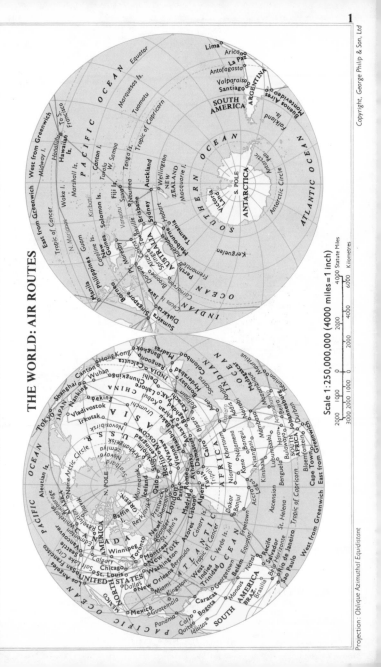

Scale 1:250,000,000 (4000 miles=1 inch)

2000 1000 0   2000   4000 Statute Miles

3000 2000 1000 0   2000   4000   6000 Kilometres

Projection: Oblique Azimuthal Equidistant

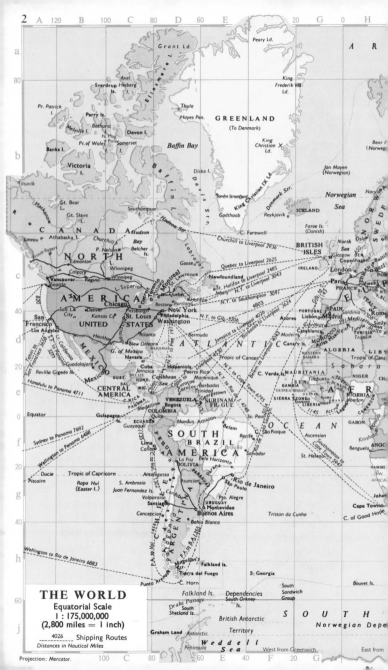

THE WORLD
Equatorial Scale
1 : 175,000,000
(2,800 miles = 1 inch)

------ 4026 Shipping Routes
Distances in Nautical Miles

Projection: Mercator.

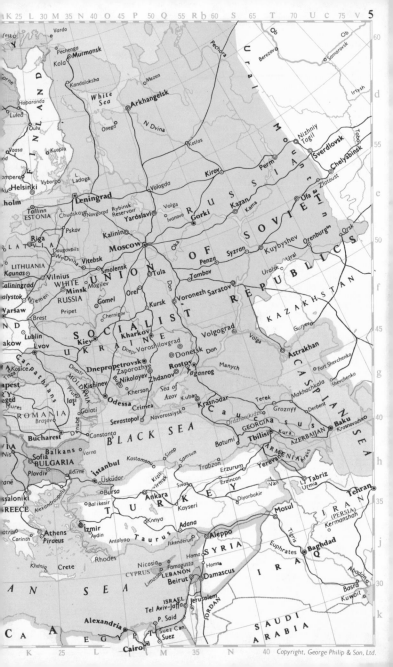

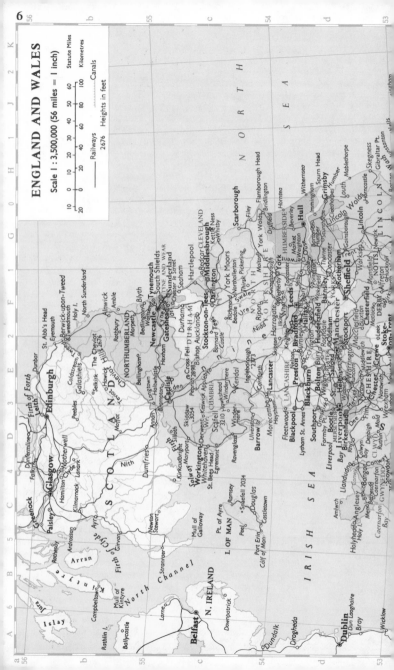

ENGLAND AND WALES

Scale 1 : 3,500,000 (56 miles = 1 inch)

Railways
Canals
Heights in feet

2676

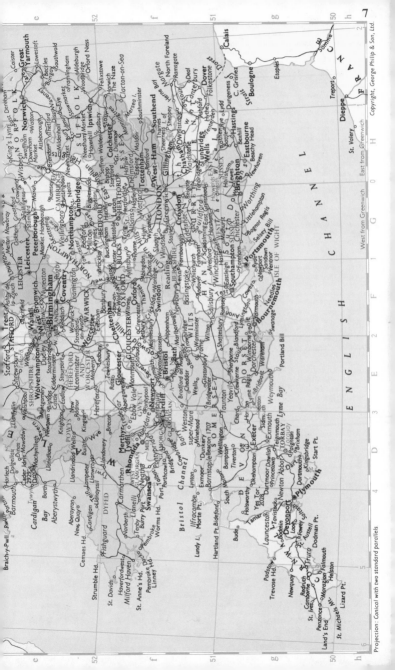

Projection: Conical with two standard parallels

SCOTLAND

Scale 1 : 3,500,000 (56 miles = 1 inch)

Railways .... Canals   3547 Heights in feet

Projection: Conical
with two standard parallels.

West from Greenwich

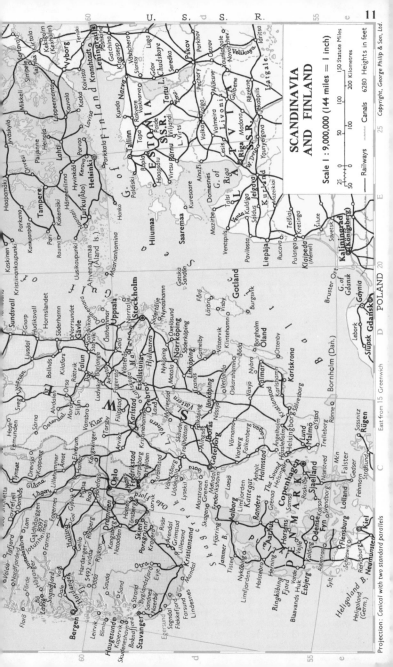

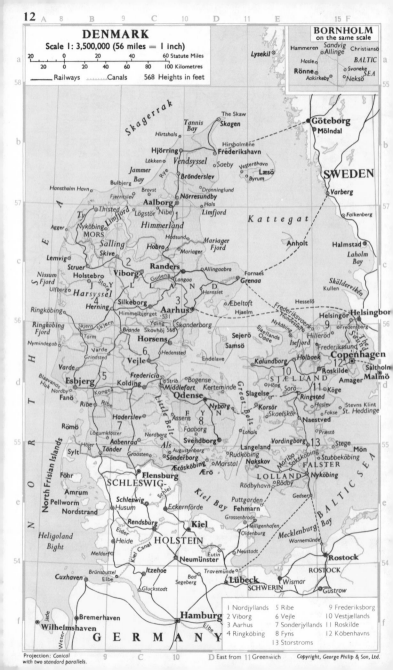

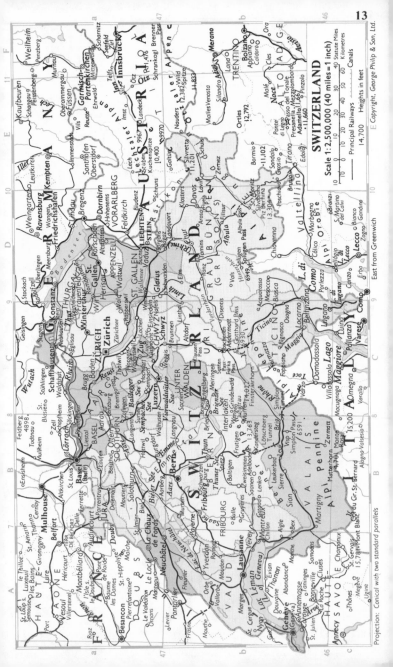

13

SWITZERLAND

Scale 1:2,500,000 (40 miles=1 inch)

Principal Railways — Canals

Heights in feet

E Copyright, George Philip & Son, Ltd.

East from Greenwich

Projection: Conical with two standard parallels

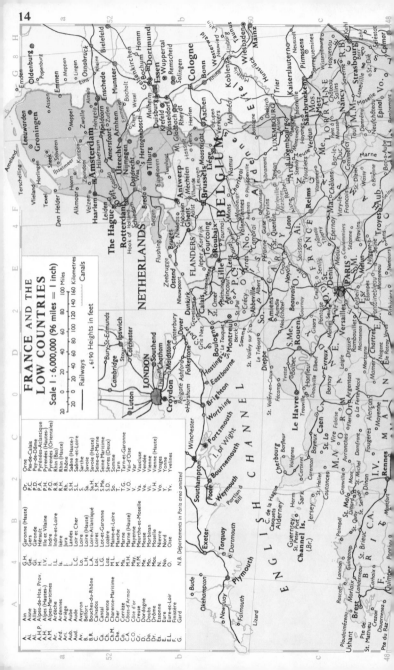

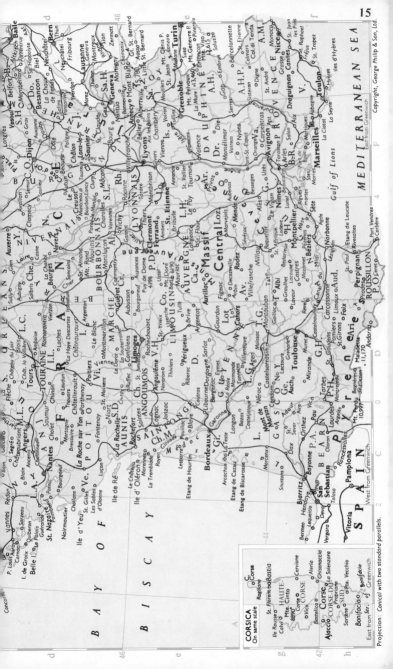

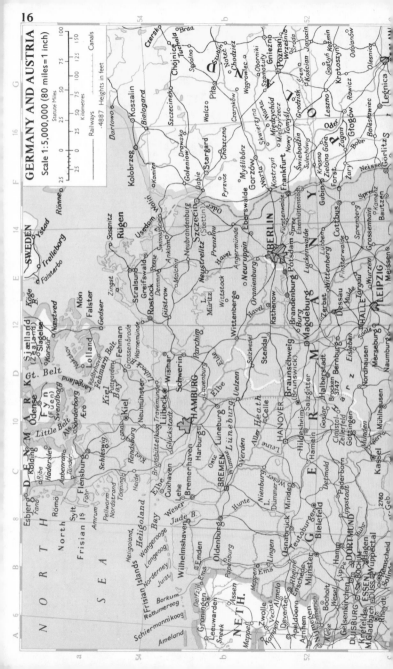

16

GERMANY AND AUSTRIA
Scale 1:5,000,000 (80 miles = 1 inch)

Statute Miles
25   0   25   50   75   100   125   150
Kilometres
25 0   25   50   75   100

Railways ———
Canals ————
-4887- Heights in feet

NORTH SEA

SWEDEN

DENMARK

NETH.

Ystad
Trelleborg
Rønne
Falsterbo
Køge B.
Mön
Falster
Skælland (Zealand)
Slagelse
Næstved
Gedser
Rødbyhavn
Lolland
Langeland
Ærø
Svendborg
Fyn (Füen)
Odense
Great Belt
Kt.
Kolding
Ribe
Haderslev
Aabenraa
Tønder
Fanø
Esbjerg
Rømø
Føhr
Amrum
Sylt
Flensburg
Schleswig
Pellworm
Nordstrand
Tönning
Heide
Husum

Czersk
Brda
Chójnice
Tuchola
Sępólno
Noteć
Obornik
Gniezno
Poznań
Września
Środa
Kościan
Śrem
Gostyń
Krotoszyn
Leszno
Rawicz
Głogów
Góra
Bolesławiec
Legnica
Neisse
Görlitz
Żary
Zielona Góra
Krosno
Zagań
Gubin
Sprey
Spremberg
Cottbus
Bautzen
Kamenz
Meissen
LEIPZIG
HALLE
Merseburg
Naumburg
Zeitz
Eisenach

Sassnitz
Rügen
Stralsund
Greifswald
Zingst
Rostock
Warnemünde
Wismar
Kiel
Fehmarn
Lübeck
HAMBURG
BREMEN
Bremerhaven
Cuxhaven
Wilhelmshaven
Emden
Oldenburg
Groningen
Leeuwarden
Assen
Zwolle
Apeldoorn
Arnhem
Nijmegen

Koszalin
Białogard
Szczecinek
Darłowo
Stargard
Goleniów
Kamień
Dąbie
Szczecin (Stettin)
Świnoujście
Wolin
Kołobrzeg
Drawsko
Czaplinek
Wałcz
Piła
Czarnków
Wągrowiec
Myślibórz
Gorzów
Kostrzyn
Frankfurt
Oder
Eberswalde
BERLIN
Potsdam
Brandenburg
Magdeburg
HANOVER
Braunschweig (Brunswick)
Wolfsburg
Salzgitter
DORTMUND
ESSEN
DUISBURG
BOCHUM
Wuppertal
Krefeld
Köln

Neisse

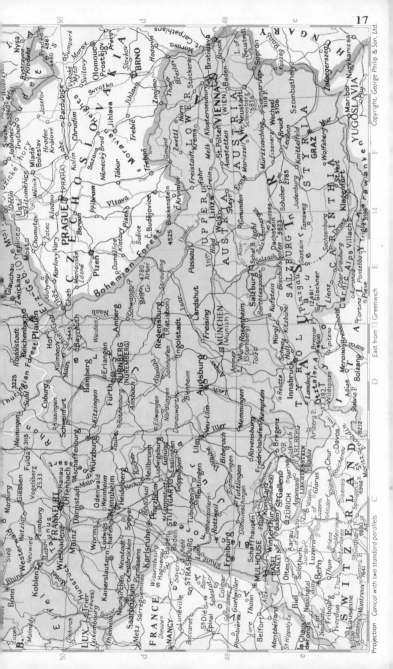

17

Projection · Conical with two standard parallels

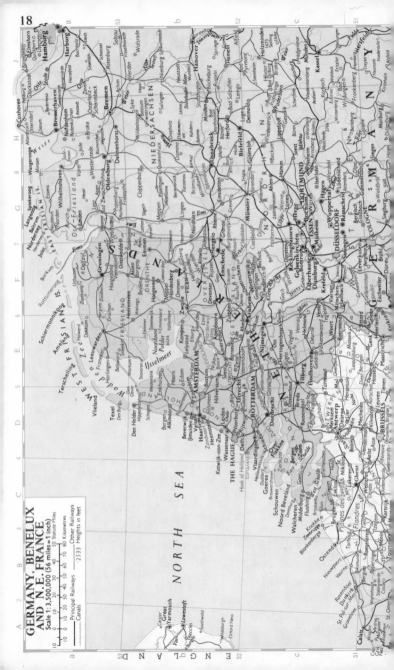

19

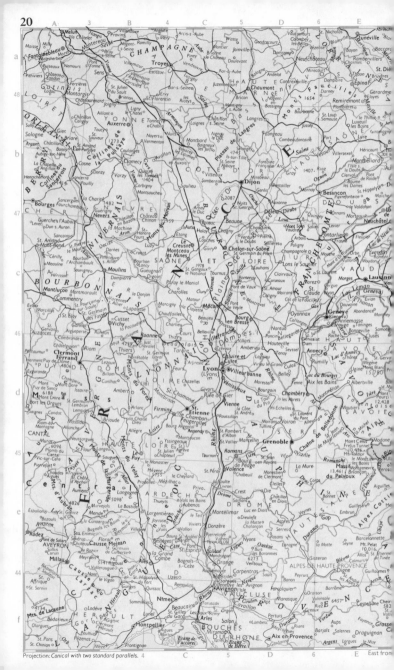

E. FRANCE, SWITZERLAND
& N.W. ITALY
Scale 1 : 3,500,000 (56 miles=1 inch)

Principal Railways ——— Other Railways
Canals   1745 Heights in feet

J. Copyright, George Philip & Son, Ltd.

BALTIC SEA

Zingst
Sassnitz
Rügen
Ustka
Wejherowo
Gdyn
Warnemünde
Stralsund
Greifswald
Darlowoo
Słupsk
Sopot
Nol
Rostock
Peene
Usedom
Kołobrzeg
Koszalin
Kartuzy
GDAN
(DAN
Güstrow
Demmin
Anklam
Swinoujście
Wolin
Białogard
Szczecinek
Tczew
Malchin
Odra Port
Kamien
Starogard
Czersk
Neubrandenburg
Goleniów
Drawsko
Choinice
Tuchola
Grudziądz
Parchim
L.
Müritz
Neustrelitz
Szczecin
(Stettin)
Dabie
Stargard
Wałcz
Piła
Bydgoszcz
(Bromberg)
Sępolno
Świecie
Chełm
Wittenberge
Wittstock
Prenzlau
Pyrzyce
Choszczno
Czarnków
Notec
Chodzież
Szubin
Toruń
Lu
Angermünde
Myślibórz
Wagrowiec
Inowrocław
Neuruppin
Havel
Eberswalde
Gorzów
Warta
Skwierzyna
Warta
Oborniki
Szamotuły
Mogilno
Płowce
Strzelno
Br
Ku
Stendal
Oranienburg
Havel
BERLIN
Fürstenwalde
Frankfurt
Kostrzyń
Międzyrzecz
Nowy Tomyśl
Gniezno
(Gnesen)
Września
Rathenow
Brandenburg
Potsdam
Spree
Luckenwalde
Świebodzin
Sulechów
Grodzisk
POZNAŃ
Słupca
Koło
Burg
Zerbst
Wittenberg
Lübben
Gubin
Krosno
Zielona Góra
POL
Śrem
Kościan
Środa
Jarocin
Konin
Turek
Łęcz
Dessau
Mulde
Finsterwalde
HALLE
Torgau
Wurzen
Cottbus
Forst
Żary
Zagań
Głogów
Leszno
Gostyń
Koźmin
Pleszew
Kalisz
Ożor
Zdun
Wol
LEIPZIG
Grossenhain
Spremberg
Kamenz
Rawicz
Krotoszyn
Ostrów
Odolanów
Ostrzeszów
Sieradz
Zeitz
Gera
Meissen
Bautzen
Bolesławiec
Kępno
Wieluń
Ra
Chemnitz
DRESDEN
Görlitz
Legnica
Oleśnica
Namysłów
Kr
Zwickau
Glauchau
Reichenbach
Geb. (Erz Mts)
Podmokly
Luban
Žittau
Liberec
Jelenia Góra
Krkonoše (Giant Mts)
Śnieżka 5260
WROCŁAW
(Breslau)
Częstochow
Plauen
Erz
Teplice
Most
Usti
Jablonec
Trutnov
Świdnica
Wałbrzych
Opole
Tarn G
Lubl
Jáchymov
Chomutov
Mittel G
Litoměřice
Hory
Mladá
Boleslav
Kłodzko
Nysa
Prudnik
Zabrze
Gliwice
Chorzów
Cheb
Karlovy Vary
Ohre
Kladno
Hradec
Králové
Josefov
Králický Sněžník
Praděd 4887
4460
Racibórz
Karviná
Biała
Mariánské
Lázně
PRAGUE (PRAHA)
Beroun
Kolín
Chrudim
Vysoké
Mýto
Šumperk
Moravská
Opava
Šternberk
Ostrava
C. Těšín
Plzeň
(Pilsen)
Příbram
Sázava
Německý Brod
Svitavy
Olomouc
Prostějov
Frýdek Místek
Nový Jičín
Jablunka P.
1810
West
Domažlice
Klatovy
Písek
Tábor
Jihlava
Přerov
Dolní
Váh
Zilin
Regen
4780
Gr. Arber
Šušice
Č. Budějovice
Třeboň
Třebíč
Jihlava
Slavkov
BRNO
Kroměříž
Gottwaldov
(Zlín)
Trenčín
Ban
By
Straubing
4525 Blöckenstein
Gmünd
Znojmo
White M
Hodonín
Kremnica
Isar
Passau
Č. Krumlov
Zwettl
Horn
Thaya
Břeclav
Morava
Trnava
Zlaté
Moravce
Nitra
Banske
UPPER
Ried
Freistadt
Urfahr
Grein
Krems
Melk
Stockerau
LOWER
Enzersdorf
Bratislava
Nové
Zámky
Ip
AUSTRIA
Wels
Linz
Steyr
St. Pölten
Amstetten
Klosterneuburg
VIENNA
(WIEN)
Baden
Bruck
Schutt
I.
Hegyeshalom
Komárno
Salzburg
Schaf b.
Attersee
Gmunden
Enns
Mariazell
Wr. Neustadt
Schnee B
6816
Enns
L. of
Neusiedl
Esztergom
Berchtesgaden
Ischl
Salzkammergut
Aussee
Mürzzuschlag
Eisenerz
Semmering
3119 F.
Sopron
Győr
Bischofshofen
9823
Dachstein

Projection: Bonne.

POLAND AND
CZECHOSLOVAKIA
Scale 1 : 5,000,000 (80 miles = 1 inch)

Railways — Canals ----- Heights in feet ·5260

East from Greenwich Copyright, George Philip & Son, Ltd.

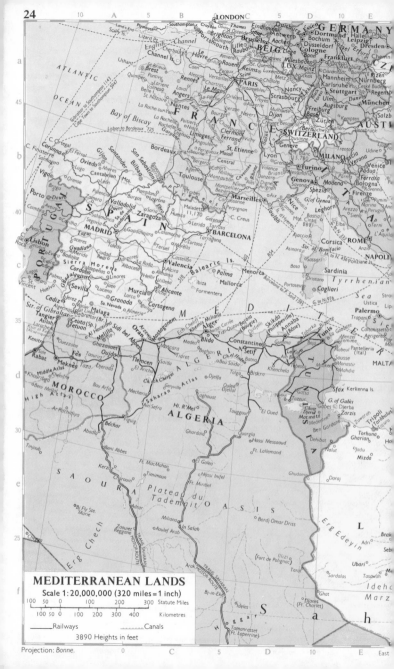

MEDITERRANEAN LANDS
Scale 1:20,000,000 (320 miles=1 inch)

100 50 0   100   200   300   Statute Miles

100 50 0   100   200   300   400   Kilometres

——— Railways   ········· Canals

3890 Heights in feet

Projection: Bonne.

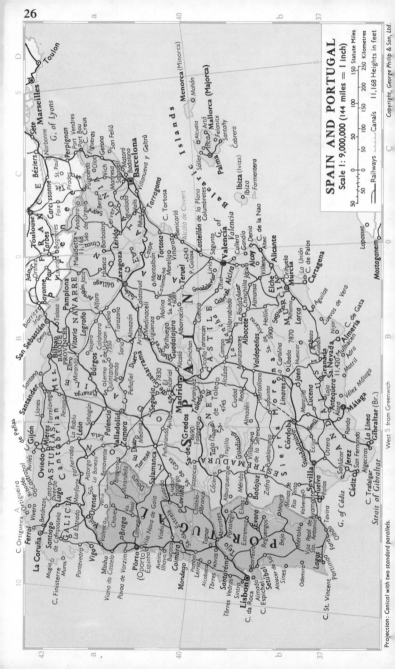

26

SPAIN AND PORTUGAL

Scale 1: 9,000,000 (144 miles = 1 inch)

Statute Miles
150

Kilometres
250

— Railways — Canals — 11,168 Heights in feet

Copyright, George Philip & Son, Ltd.

Projection: Conical with two standard parallels.

West 5 from Greenwich

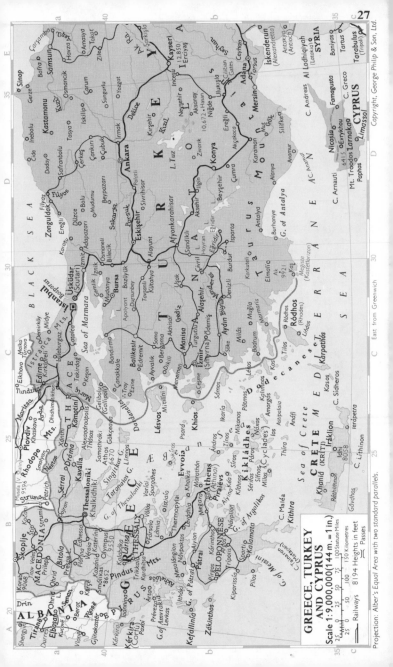

27

GREECE, TURKEY
AND CYPRUS
Scale 1:9,000,000 (144 m. = 1 in.)

| 25 | 0 | 25 | 50 | 75 | 100 Statute Miles |
| 25 | 0 | 50 | 100 | 150 Kilometres |

━━━ Railways   8194 Heights in feet   )(Passes

Projection: Alber's Equal Area with two standard parallels.

Copyright, George Philip & Son. Ltd.

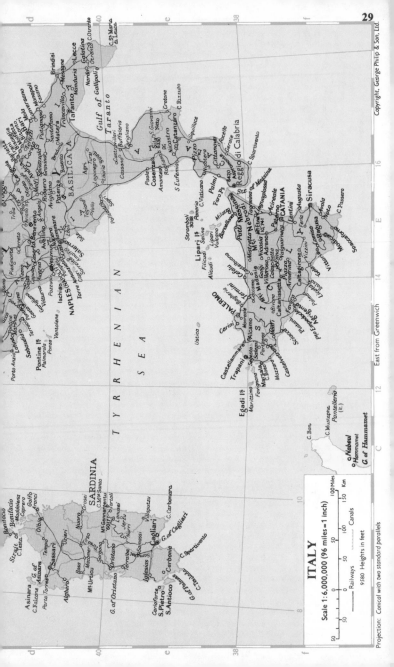

29

Copyright, George Philip & Son, Ltd.

East from Greenwich

ITALY

Scale 1:6,000,000 (96 miles=1 inch)

Railways ——— Canals - - - -

9,580 Heights in feet

Projection: Conical with two standard parallels

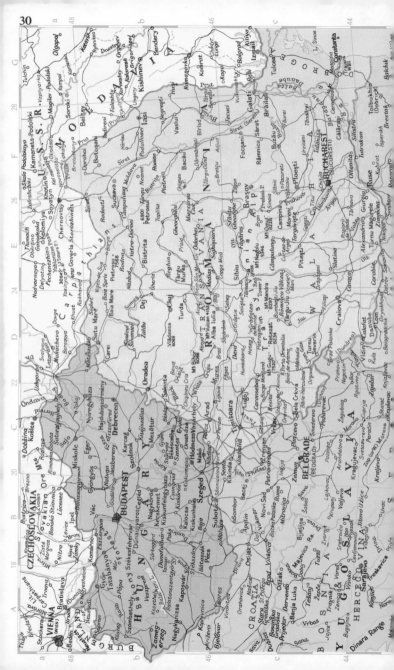

31

HUNGARY AND
THE BALKAN STATES
Scale 1:6,000,000 (96 miles = 1 inch)

Statute Miles
25   50   100   150

Kilometres
25 50   100   150

Railways ········ Canals
▲ 8300 Heights in feet

Copyright, George Philip & Son, Ltd.

Projection: Conical with two standard parallels

East from 24°Greenwich

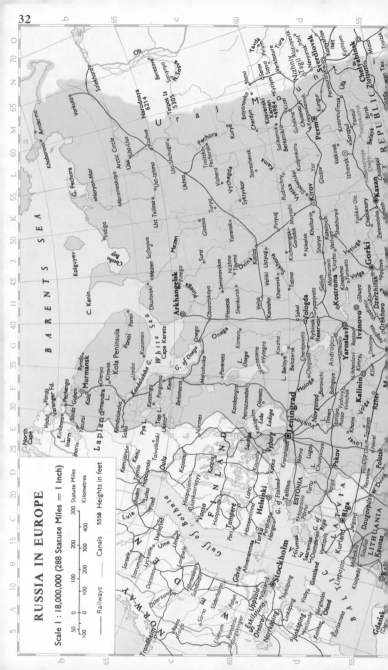

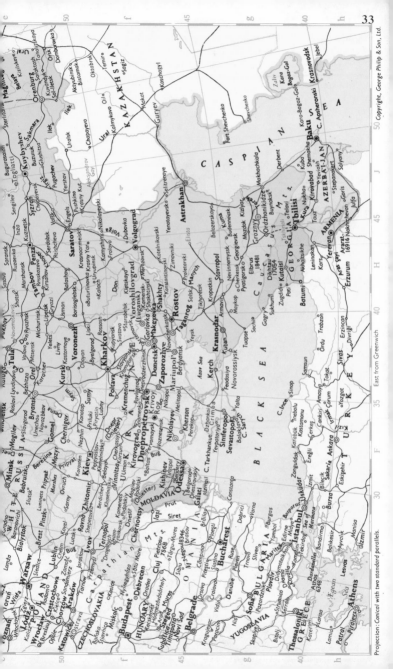

33

Projection: Conical with two standard parallels.

East from Greenwich

West from Greenwich

ICELAND

ATLANTIC
OCEAN

ARCTIC

Jan Mayen

Svalbard

Franz Josef Land

BRITISH
ISLES

Bergen
Trondheim
North Cape
Hammerfest

NORWAY

Barents
Sea

Novaya Zemlya

Kara
Sea

North
Sea

DENMARK

Oslo

Narvik

Putih I.
Dickson

Esbjerg

SWEDEN

Murmansk
Kolguyev
Pechora
Gulf

Vaigach I.
Khabarovo

Hamburg
Berlin

Copenhagen
Malmö
Stockholm
Uppsala
Gulf of Bothnia

Kola Pen.
Kandalaksha

White
Sea

Novy Port
Vorkuta

Gulf of Ob

Se
Z

POLAND
Szczecin
Stettin

Baltic
Sea
Kaliningrad

Helsinki
Riga
Tallinn

FINLAND
Tampere
Turku

Kem
L. Onega

Arkhangelsk

Narayan Mar

Pechora

Taz

Wroclaw
Łódź
Warsaw
Warszawa

LITHUANIA
Vilnius
Minsk

Leningrad
Andropov
Ladoga

Petrozavodsk

N. Dvina

15214

West

Kraków
Brest

BELORUSSIA
Gomel

Yaroslavl
Moscow
Vitebsk
Smolensk

Vologda
Kostroma

RUSSIAN

Telposi Iz
5305

SOVIET
FEDE

Siberian

UKRAINE
Zhitomir
Kiev
Dnepropetrovsk

Orel
Tula
Ryazan
Tambov

Ivanovo
Gorki
Ulyanovsk

Izhevsk
Kirov
Berezniki

Serov

Plain

Nizhniy Tagil

Chernovtsy
Kishinev

Krivoy Rog
Nikolayev

Kharkov
Voronezh
Saratov
Penza

Kazan
Ufa

Perm

Tyumen
Tobolsk

Irtysh

Simferopol
Odessa
Sevastopol

Zaporozhye
Donetsk
Makeyevka
Rostov

Volgograd
Engels

Kuybyshev
Chapayevsk

Zlatoust
Kam

Sverdlovsk
Chelyabinsk

Petropavlovsk

S

Tomsk

Black Sea
Samsun
Trabzon
Batumi

Krasnodar
Maikop
Shakhty

Don

Astrakhan

Ural
Uralsk
Orenburg
Orsk

Kurgan
Magnitogorsk

Omsk
Tatarsk
Novosibirsk

Barnaul

TURKEY
Erzurum

Leninakan
Tbilisi
GEORGIA
Grozny

Caspian
Sea

Guryev

K
A
Z

Aktyubinsk

Tselinograd
Pavlodar

Slavgorod

Biy

Lenine

Diyarbakir
L. Urmia

AZERBAIJAN
Yerevan
Baku

Krasnovodsk

Ust Urt Plateau

KIRGIZ

Karaganda
Karsakpai

Semipalatinsk

Ayaguz

Belu
15,15

Mosul
IRAQ
Kirkuk

Tabriz
Rasht

Ashkhabad

Aral
Sea

Syr Darya

Kzyl Orda

L. Balkhash

Balkhash

Dzhambul

Tahche

Baghdad
Euphrates
Hamadan

Tehran

Bandar Turkmen

TURKMENISTAN

Kara Kum
Khiva
Amu Darya

Kyzyl Kum

Bukhara
Chardzhou

UZBEKISTAN
Tashkent
Chimkent

Leninabad

Frunze
Namangan
Andizhan
Kokand

Alma Ata

Kuldja

KIRGIZIA
Przhevalsk
Pobeda Pk.
24,406

SINK

UIG

Basra
Abadan
Kuwait

The
Gulf

Bushire

IRAN
Esfahan
Yazd
Shiraz

Mashhad

Mary

Samarkand
TADZHIKISTAN
Dushanbe

Termez

Communism
24,590

Pamirs

Khan Tengri 22,9

Kashgar
Tarim

Yarkand

Takla Ma

SINK

Kerman

Herat

AFGHANISTAN

Mazar-i-Sharif

Shghr-i-Zabul

PAKISTAN

Kashmir

Khotan

TIB

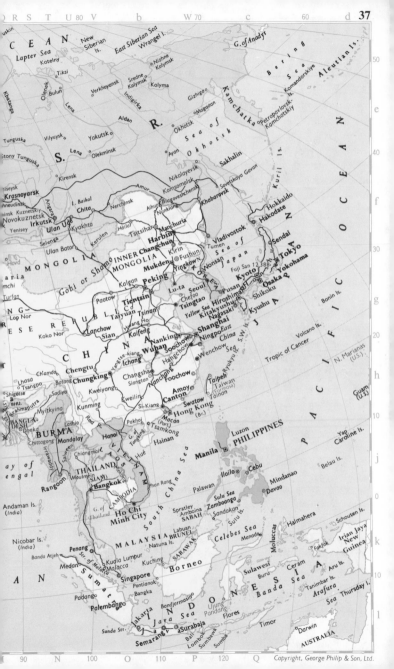

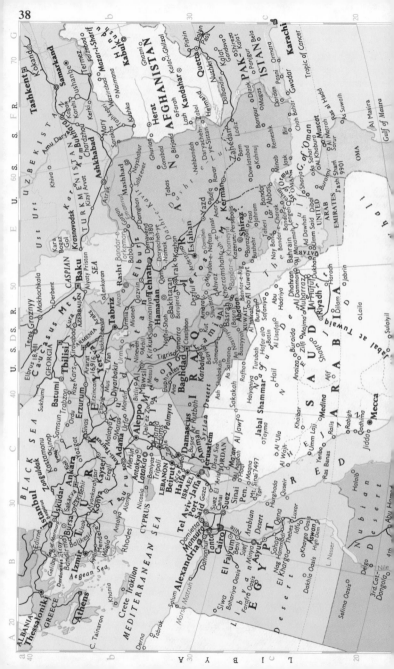

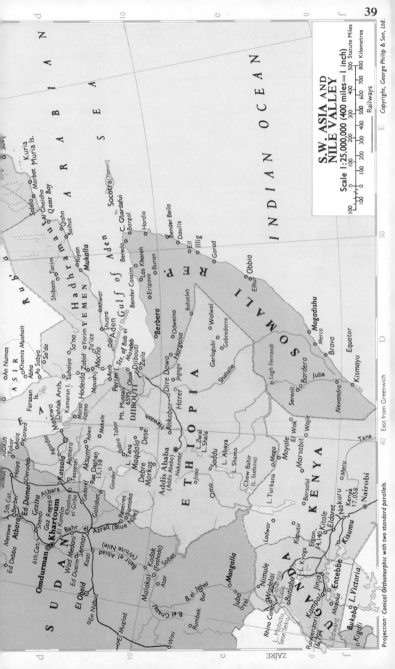

39

S.W. ASIA AND
NILE VALLEY

Scale 1:25,000,000 (400 miles = 1 inch)

Railways

Copyright, George Philip & Son, Ltd.

Projection: Conical Orthomorphic with two standard parallels.

THE LEVANT

Scale 1:4,000,000
(64 miles=1 inch)

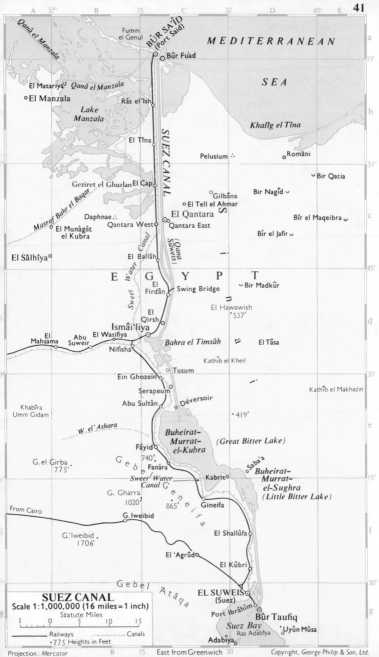

SUEZ CANAL

MEDITERRANEAN SEA

Qanâ el Manzala

Fumm el Genul
BÛR SAÏD (Port Saïd)
Bûr Fuàd

El Matarîya
Qanâ el Manzala
El Manzala
Râs el 'Ish
Lake Manzala

Khalîg el Tîna

El Tîna

Geziret el Ghuzlan
El Cap
Pelusium ∴
Români

Bir Qatia

Gilbâna
El Tell el Ahmar
Bir Nagîd

Bîr el Maqeibra

Daphnae ∴
Qantara West
El Qantara
Qantara East

Bîr el Jafîr

Masraf Bahr el Baqar
El Munâgât el Kubra

El Sâlhîya
El Ballâh

E G Y P T

El Firdân
Swing Bridge
Bir Madkûr

El Qirsh
El Hawawish '537'

Ismâi'liya
El Mahsama
Abu Suweir
El Wasifiya
Bahra el Timsâh
El Tâsa
Nifisha
Kathîb el Kheil
Tusum

Ein Ghozein
Kathîb el Makhazin

Serapeum
Déversoir
Abu Sultân

Khabîra Umm Gidam

'419'

W. el 'Ashara

Buheirat-Murrat-el-Kubra
(Great Bitter Lake)

Fâyid
G. el Girbâ '775'
740'
Fanâra
Sweet Water Canal
Sabâ'a
Kabrit
Buheirat-Murrat-el-Sughra
(Little Bitter Lake)

G. Gharra 1020'
865'
Gineifa

From Cairo
G. Iweibid

G. Iweibid 1706'
El Shallûfa

El 'Agrûd
El Kûbri

Gebel 'Atâqa

EL SUWEIS (Suez)
Port Ibrâhîm
Bûr Taufiq
Suez Bay
Ras Adabîya
Adabîya
Uyûn Mûsa

SUEZ CANAL
Scale 1:1,000,000 (16 miles = 1 inch)
Statute Miles
5   10   15

—— Railways   Canals
•775 Heights in Feet

Projection : Mercator   East from Greenwich   Copyright, George Philip & Son, Ltd.

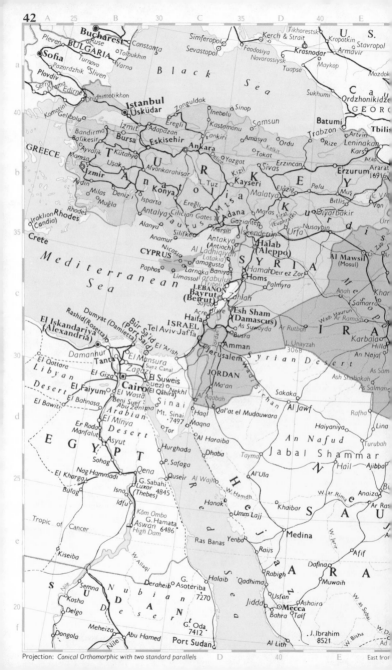

CENTRAL MIDDLE EAST COUNTRIES

Scale 1:17,500,000 (280 miles=1 inch)

Statute Miles
100 50 0   100   200   300

100 50 0   100   200   300   400   500
Kilometres

———— Railways   ———— Principal Roads

·7350 Heights in feet – – – – Caravan Routes and Tracks

Copyright, George Philip & Son, Ltd.

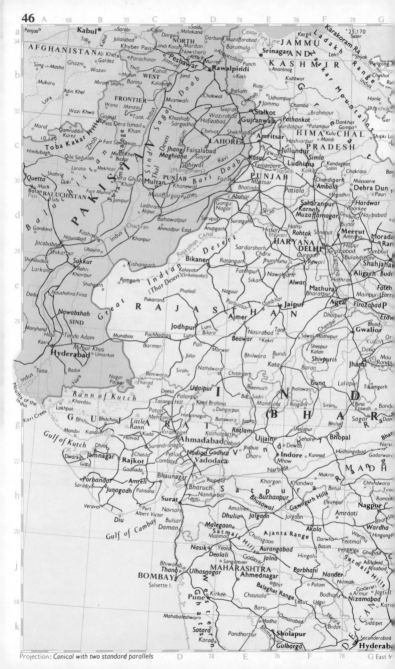

INDO-GANGETIC PLAIN

Scale 1:12,000,000 (192 miles = 1 inch)

| 50 | 0 | 50 | 100 | 150 | 200 Statute Miles |
| 50 | 0 | 50 | 100 | 150 | 200 | 250 | 300 Kilometres |

—— Railways ‥‥‥ Canals 11,200 Heights in feet

47

PEOPLE'S REPUBLIC OF CHINA

T I B E T

Kashum Tso

Aling Kangri 24,000
or Senge Khambab

Shazia

Nagrong

Jiachan

Selipuk Gompa

Wampo

Ed Dzong

Shaba Gomba

Zilling Tso

Nogchu Dzong

K a n g r i

Tangra Tso

Kyaring Tso

Nam Tso

Shentsa

23,255

N y e n c h e n   T a n g l h a

Phongda

Mendong Gompa

Lingakok

Matsang (Tsangpo)

Lhasa

Rakas Lake

Gurla Mandhata 25,355

Manasarovar Lake

chen Khambab

Mayum La

Simikot

Tradom

Saka

Shigatse

Matsang or Tsum

Lhotse Dzong

Gyangtse

Tigu

Lhuntse Dzong

Mugu

Namja Pass 16,220

Mustang

Tamchok

Gya Pass 18,380

Phung Chu

Shekar Dzong

Khamba Dzong

Dhama Dzong

Tsona Dzong

Baitadi

Dandeldhura

Silgarhi Doti

Jumla

Muktinath

Gosainthan 26,291

Tindzhe Dzong

Thunkar

Karnali

Dhaulagiri 26,810

Nyalam Dz.

Mt. Everest 29,028

Kanchenjunga 28,165

R a n g e

Towang

Dhangarhi

Nepalganj

Nuwakot

Gurkha

Katmandu

Ramechhap

Sun Kosi

Punakha

Gangtok

BHUTAN

Mongar Dzong

Lakhimpur

Jarwa

Nautanwa

Chapoli Garhi

Ilam

Darjeeling

SIKKIM

Taga-Dzong

UTTAR

Sitapur

Bahraich

Balrampur

Thori

Birganj

Dhankuta

Siliguri

Jainti

Alipur Duar

Cooch Behar

Rangia

ASSAM

Gonda

Basti

Bettiah

Jalpaiguri

W. BENGAL

Barpeta

Goalpara

Gauhati

Lucknow

Rae Bareli

Faizabad

Gorakhpur

Deoria

Motihari

Jaynagar

Kishanganj

Purnea

Dhubri

Tura

MEGHALAYA

Shillong

Kanpur

Unnao

Sultanpur

Azamgarh

Ghaghra

Siwan

Chapra

Darbhanga

Nirmali

Supaul

Katihar

Dinajpur

Rangpur

Cherrapunji

DESH

Allahabad

Fatehpur

Jaunpur

Ghazipur

Patna

Bankipore

Muzaffarpur

Biharigani

Sahibganj

RAJSHAHI

Bogra

Jamalpur

Mohanganj

Sylhet

Bela

Varanasi (Benares)

Mirzapur

Sasaram

Arrah

Jahanabad

Bihar

Jamalpur

Monghyr

Bhagalpur

Tinpahar

English Bazar

Nasirabad

Netrakona

Mymensingh

Karimganj

Banda

Maihar

Mauganj

Gaya

Aurangabad

Barhi

Giridih

Rampur Hat

Berhampore

Nabadwip

Rajshahi

Pabna

Kushtia

Naogaon

Kishorganj

Dacca

Narayanganj

DHAKA

TRIPURA

Agartala

Amarpur

Belonia

Satna

Rewa

Dudhi

Hazaribagh

Ramgarh

Damodar

Dhanbad

Asansol

Raniganj

Burdwan

Krishnagar

Runaghat

Madaripur

Comilla

Murwara

Umaria

Shahdol

Chirimiri

Bharatpur

Ambikapur

Lohardaga

Ranchi

Purulia

Bankura

Serampore

Barrackpore

CALCUTTA

Jessore

Khulna

Barisal

Bhola

Maijdi (Noakhali)

Hatia I.

Nazir Hat

Chittagong

balpur

Anuppur

Bilaspur

Chakradharpur

Jamshedpur

Chaibasa

Midnapore

Howrah

Kharagpur

Diamond Harbour

Port Canning

Sundarbans

Ganga

Mandla

Nainpur

PRADESH

Kawardha

Bilaspur

Sundargarh

Bimitrapur

Gua

Badampahar

Baripada

Contai

Holdia

the

Mouths of

Ghata R.

Sandwip

Balaghat

Khairagarh

Raigarh

Jharsuguda

Sambalpur

Keonjhar

Balasore

Subarnarekha

Raipur

Sarangarh

Talcher

Brahmani

Bhadrakh

Dhamtari

Drug

Sonepur

Mahanadi

Dhenkanal

Kendrapara

Kanker

Balangir

O R I S S A

Cuttack

Mahanadi

Bhubaneswar

Bhawanipatna

Russellkonda

Chilka Lake

Puri

Bhanragarh (Indravati)

Bastar

Rayagada

Berhampur

Chatrapur

Ichhapuram

Bijapur

Jagdalpur

Jeypore

Koraput

Parvatipuram

Tekkali

Srikakulam

Venkatapuram

Kontar

Salur

Bobbili

Northern Circars

4466

Vizianagaram

Kottagudem

Andakapalle

hammom

Vishakhapatnam

E a s t e r n   G h a t s

eenwich

Copyright, George Philip & Son, Ltd.

EAST INDIES
AND
FURTHER INDIA
Scale 1:25,000,000
(400 miles = 1 inch)

100 50 0   100   200   300 Statute Miles
100 50 0   100 200 300 400 500 Kilometres
Railways   Canals
▲ 9612 Heights in feet

Projection: Conical

BURMA
(MYANMAR)
YUNNAN
CHINA
KWEICHOW
KWANGSI-
CHUANG
KWANGTUNG
Kunming
Canton
Macao

Mandalay
Mayo
Hanoi
Haiphong
Gulf of Tonking
Hainan
Hoihow

Prome
Chiang Mai
Vientiane
THAILAND
(SIAM)

Rangoon
Moulmein
BANGKOK
Ayutthaya

Bassein

Andaman
Sea

Mergui
Archipelago

Tavoy

Isthmus of Kra

CAMBODIA
Pnom Penh

VIETNAM
Da-Nang (Tourane)
Hué
Quang Ngai
Binh Dinh
Nha Trang
Phan Rang
Phan Thiet
HO CHI MINH CITY
Bien Hoa

Paracel Is.
(S. Vietnam)

SOUTH CHINA
SEA

Spratly I.
Amboyna Cay

Phuket
Surat Thani

Gulf of
Thailand

George Town
Penang
Ipoh
PENINSULAR
MALAYSIA
Kuala Lumpur
Malacca
Johore Bahru
SINGAPORE

Kota Bharu

MALAYSIA

BRUNEI
Bandar Seri Begawan
SARAWAK
Kuching

SUMATRA
Medan
Padang
Palembang

BORNEO
KALIMANTAN

Great
Channel

INDIAN
OCEAN

INDONESIA

JAKARTA
Bogor
Bandung
Semarang
Surabaya
Jogjakarta
Surakarta
Malang

Greater Sunda
Madura
Bali

Preparis

Continuation Eastwards
on same scale

PACIFIC OCEAN

Dampier Str. Sorong Waibeem Kairoini Manokwari
Salmono Klamono
Vogelkop
Sailolo Klamono
Misool Bira Wasian Wariap Japen Str.
CERAM McCluer Gulf Geelvink
SEA Fakfak Bay
Kaimana IRIAN JAYA Snow Mountain
Wandiri Nassau 16,400
Mimika Mts. 15,400

Schouten Is.
C. d'Urville
Japen Nuboai
Ansoedoe
Moeris
Djajapura
Vanimo
Aitape Wewak
Sepik R. Manam
PAPUA
NEW
GUINEA Muller Ra. 15,400
Strickland
Kikori
NEW Awonno
Kai Is.
Aru GUINEA Gulf of
Is. Papua
Tanimbar Is. Flamingo B. Tanamerah
Jamdena Kolepom I. Okaba Daru
Merauke Torres Strait

A R A F U R A   S E A

PHILIPPINES region (left):

FU KIEN
Santuao Foochow
Hinghwa Hinghwa
Amoy Keelung
Formosa Taipeh
Swatow Taichung
Tainan Taiwan (Formosa)
Kaohsiung Hualien
Pingtung Taitung
Tropic of Cancer Huotsao Tao
Hungtou Hsu (Lan Yu)
Y'Ami Hengchun
Pratas Batan Is.
(China) Basco
Balingtang
Balintang Channel
Babuyan Is.
Negra Pt. Aparri Babuyan I.
Laoag Claveria Camiguin
Batac Engaño
C. Bolinao Vigan Tuguegarao Palanan
San Fernando Bongued
Lingayen Bontoc 961
Lingayen G. Baguio C. San
Dasupan Idefonso
Cabanatuan
C. Bolinao Tarlac Quezon City
San Fernando Manila
Manila B. Bataan San Pablo Daet Catanduanes
Lubang Is. Cavite Lucena Naga Yog Pt.
Batangas Boac Calauag Virac
Calapan Legaspi Sorsogon
Mindoro Mindoro Str. Looc Masbate Gubat
Busuanga Cuyo Pandan Calbayog Samar
Calamian Group Roxas (Capiz) Catarman
Bacuit Iloilo Panay Catbalogan
Tablas Cebu Leyte
San Jose Bayvay
Dumaran Negros Bacolod Cebu Bohol
Palawan Puerto Princesa Dumaguete Siargao
Mt. Mantalingajan Tanjay Tandag
6839 Tubbataha Talisayan Lianga
Reefs Mondho Cagayan San Juan
Bugsuk Iligan Malaybalay
Balabac Cagayan Pagadian Mindanao
Banggi Sulu Ozamiz Davao
Turtle Is. Zamboanga Dulawan Apo 9690
Kinabalu Pangutaran Lamitan Digos
13,455 Group Jolo Basilan Cotabato Davao
Sandakan Tinaca Pt.
Pintosan Lahad Datu Tawitawi Is. Sibutu Nenusa Is.

Sulu Sea
Sulu Arch.

PACIFIC OCEAN
Caroline Is.
Belau Koror
Sonsorol Is.
Pulo Anna
Merir
Tobi

Celebes Sea region (bottom):

St. Lucia B. Tahuna Sangihe Is.
Bunju Tarakan Siau Pitu
Tandjung Selor Kemul Sangihe Morotai
Marutua Galela
Kajan Batuputih Manado Klabat Maju Halmahera
Tolitoli 6545 Djailolo Asia Is.
Amurang Ternate Buli Aju Is. Equator
Mangkalihat Poeleh Kotabunu Gotowasi Waibeem
Sangkulirang Tomini 6430 Patani Wokre Sorong
Muara-Antjalung Togian Is. Gorontalo Gani Samate Vogelkop Magokwari
Bontang Tinombo Luwuk (Penju) Labuha Wersar Mogoi Wariap
Samarindo Donggala Parigi Peleng MOLUCCAS Soa Misool McCluer G.
Balikpapan Lariang Poso Banggai Taliabu Obi Obi
SULAWESI Banggai Is. Sula Is. Sanana Ceram Sea Bula Waru Fakfak Kaimana
Balangan (CELEBES) Tolo Mangole Wahai
Balambang Masamba Namlea Waru
Mamuju L. Towuti Wamlana Buru Tehuru Geser Gorong Is.
Madjene Salabangka Is. Leksula Saparua
Palopo Kendari Ambelau Ambon Banda Sea Watubela Is.
Rantekombola Manui Bandanaira Adi
11,335 Penju Is. Manuk Ewab Is.(Kai)
Ujung Pandang Maros Parepare Gulf of Bone Butung Serua Kai Ketjil Elat Tual
Tanahdjampea Wangiwangi Lucipara Is. Elat Tanimbar
Takalar Bonthain (Benteng) Tukangbesi Is. Nila Is. West Dajak Larat
Salajar Muna Pasarwadjo Bonegato Gunungapi Teun South Dais
Postiljon Is. Kalaotoa Banda Sea Damar Tepa Babar Jamdena
Nusa Tenggara (Lesser Sunda Is.) Flores Nova Sagres Sermata Selaru
Sumbawa Membaro Rote Sawu Kisar Moa Soumlaki
Ende Geliting Pantai Dili Baucau (Va. Salazar) Arafura
Waingapu Sawu Sea Alor Atauro Vila Nova de Malaca Sea
Sumba Sumba Ataupu Ossusi Armindo Monteiro
4019 Seba Kupang Timor C. Van Diemen Melville
Lesser Sunda Is. Savu Sea Roti Timor Sea Bathurst I. AUSTRALIA

ARAFURA SEA

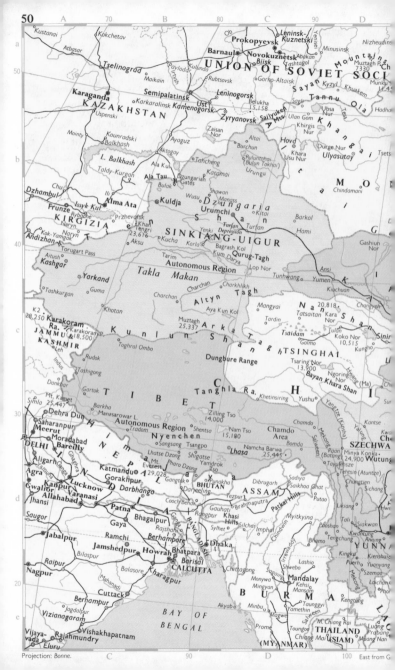

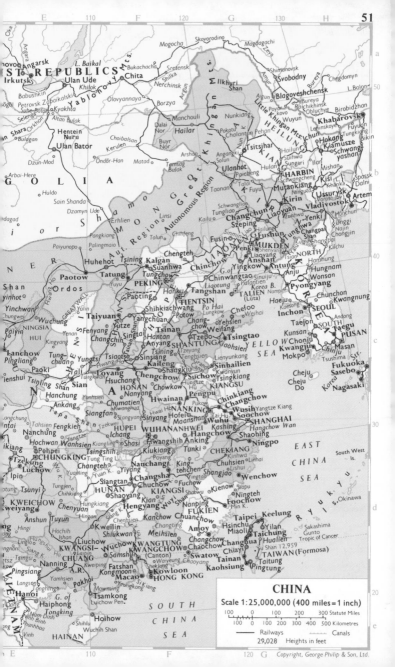

CHINA

Scale 1:25,000,000 (400 miles = 1 inch)

100   0   100   200   300 Statute Miles
100   0   100   200   300   400   500 Kilometres

—— Railways
- - - Canals
29,028   Heights in feet

Copyright, George Philip & Son, Ltd.

A   120   B   130

INNER
MONGOLIA
(Autonomous Region)

Linsi

Wengniu

Chihfeng

Lunghwa Chienping

Chengteh

HOPEI

Tsunhwa

Tangshan Changli

Chinwangtao

Hanku

Po Hai
(G. of Chihli)

Haung
Ho

Weifang

SHANTUNG

Chuhsien

Lienyunkang
Sinhailien

Kwanyun

Tsingkiang

Paoying Yencheng

KIANGSU

Kaoyu

Yangchow Taichow

Chinkiang

Changchow Nantung

Wusih Tai
Hu

Soochow

Huchow Sunkiang

SHANGHAI

Hangchow

Hangchow Wan

Kienteh Tinghai

Kinhwa Shaohing Fenghwa Ningpo

Lishui Linhai Shihpu

CHEKIANG

Wenchow

EAST CHINA
SEA

Taichintala Paicheng

Taonan Talai Shwangcheng Hulan Payen Ilan

Kaitung Fuyu Lalin HARBIN Fangcheng

Nungan Wuchang Imienpo Mutankiang

Tungliao Changchun Shwangliao Shulan Ninguta Tungning

Kailu Kungchuling Kirin Hweinan Tunwha Wangching

Kulunkai Szeping Liaoyuan Hailung Yenki Hunchun

Changwu Chngtu Tiehling Sungari Res. Hoeryong Musan

Sinmin Fushun Tunghwa Linkiang Unggi Najin Nanam

Fusin MUKDEN (Shenyang) Hwanjen Changpai Shan Chongjin

Hsihsien Penki Tsian Kilchu

Chinchow Liaoyang Panshan Kwentien Tanchon

Yingkow Anshan NORTH Hamhung

Tashihkiao Kaiping Fengcheng Antung

Hiungyeh Liaotung Pen. Sinuiju Hungnam

Fuchow Kushan Anju KOREA

Pulantien Ching-ho Pyongyang Wonsan

Lüshun TALIEN (Lüta) Korea B. Nampo Kosong

Lungkow Sariwon Sinmak Chorwon Cease Fire Line July 27, 1953

Chefoo Weihai Haeju Kaesong Chunchon Kasong

Mowping Tsingtao Inchon SEOUL Samchok

Haiyang Shihtao Suwon Chungju

YELLOW Chonan Wonju Andong

SEA SOUTH Taejon Kunchon

Kunsan Chonju Yongdong Kyongju

Chinju Taegu Miryang

Kwangju Mokpo Chinju Masan PUSAN

Posu Tsushima KOREA

Cheju Cheju Do (Quelpart)

Shimonoseki Yamaguchi HIROSH

KITAKYŪSHŪ Bofu Mat

Fukuoka Beppu Oi

Sasebo Kurume Omuta KUMAMOTO Yatsushiro N

Nagasaki Kyūshū Sendai Kobayashi Miya

Kagoshima Miyakor Kanoya Miyazaki

Tanega Sh

South-West Islands

Amami O Shima

Projection: Bonne   B   130

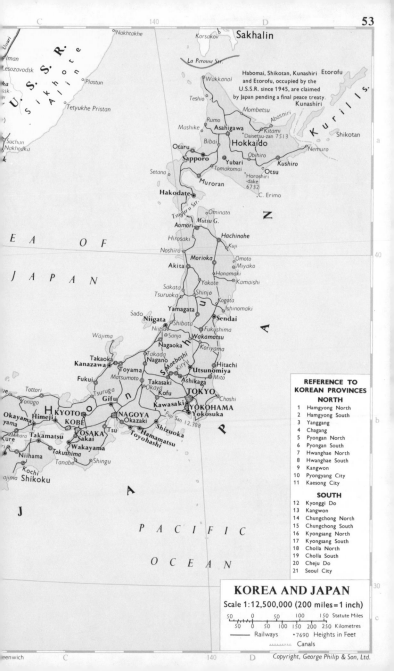

53

Sakhalin

Nakhtakhe

Korsakov

La Perouse Str.

Habomai, Shikotan, Kunashiri
and Etorofu, occupied by the
U.S.S.R. since 1945, are claimed
by Japan pending a final peace treaty.

Etorofu

Kunashiri

Kuril Is.

Shikotan

Wakkanai

Teshio

Mombetsu

Abashiri

Nemuro

Mashike

Rumoi

Kitami

Asahigawa

Daisetsu-zan 7513

Hokkaido

Otaru

Bibai

Obihiro

Sapporo

Yubari

Kushiro

Otsu

Setana

Tomakomai

*Horoshiri
-dake
6732*

Muroran

C. Erimo

Hakodate

Tsugaru Str.

Ominato

Aomori

Mutsu G.

Hirosaki

Hachinohe

Noshiro

Kuji

Morioka

Omoto

Miyako

Akita

Hanamaki

Kamaishi

Sakata

Yokote

Tsuruoka

Shinjo

Sado

Yamagata

Kogota

Ishinomaki

Niigata

Shibata

Sendai

Niitsu

Sanjo

Fukushima

Nagaoka

Wakamatsu

Wajima

Takada

Koriyama

Nagano

Maebashi

Takaoka

Matsumoto

Kiryu

Hitachi

Kanazawa

Toyama

Ashikaga

Utsunomiya

Fukui

Okaya

Mito

Tsuruga

Kofu

TOKYO

Gifu

Choshi

NAGOYA

Kawasaki

Tottori

Okazaki

Shizuoka

YOKOHAMA

Yonago

Fuji San 12,388

Yokosuka

KYOTO

KOBE

Tsu

Hamamatsu

Okayama

Himeji

Toyohashi

yama

OSAKA

Sakai

Takamatsu

Wakayama

Mihara

Tokushima

Kure

Niihama

Tanabe

Shingu

Kochi

ojima

Shikoku

SEA OF JAPAN

PACIFIC OCEAN

U.S.S.R.

Sikhote Alin

Iman

Lesozavodsk

Plastun

ssk

Tetyukhe Pristan

Suchan

Nakhodka

**REFERENCE TO
KOREAN PROVINCES**

NORTH

1	Hamgyong North
2	Hamgyong South
3	Yanggang
4	Chagang
5	Pyongan North
6	Pyongan South
7	Hwanghae North
8	Hwanghae South
9	Kangwon
10	Pyongyang City
11	Kaesong City

SOUTH

12	Kyonggi Do
13	Kangwon
14	Chungchong North
15	Chungchong South
16	Kyongsang North
17	Kyongsang South
18	Cholla North
19	Cholla South
20	Cheju Do
21	Seoul City

KOREA AND JAPAN

Scale 1:12,500,000 (200 miles=1 inch)

50   0   50   100   150 Statute Miles

50 0 50 100 150 200 250 Kilometres

——— Railways   •7690 Heights in Feet

~~~~~~ Canals

Greenwich

Copyright, George Philip & Son, Ltd.

54

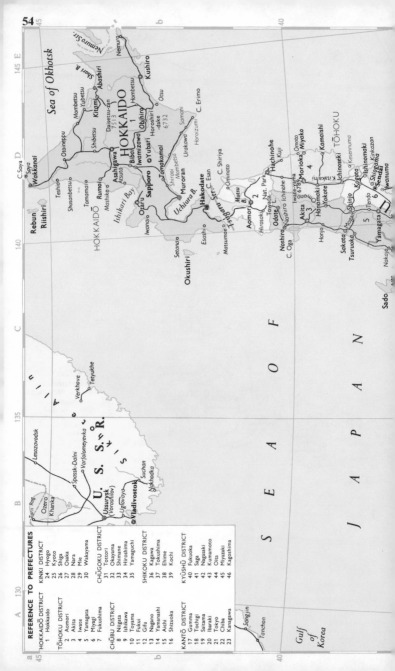

REFERENCE TO PREFECTURES

HOKKAIDŌ DISTRICT
1 Hokkaido

TŌHOKU DISTRICT
2 Aomori
3 Akita
4 Iwate
5 Yamagata
6 Miyagi
7 Fukushima

CHŪBU DISTRICT
8 Niigata
9 Ishikawa
10 Toyama
11 Fukui
12 Gifu
13 Nagano
14 Yamanashi
15 Aichi
16 Shizuoka

KANTŌ DISTRICT
17 Gumma
18 Tochigi
19 Saitama
20 Ibaraki
21 Tokyo
22 Chiba
23 Kanagawa

KINKI DISTRICT
24 Hyogo
25 Kyoto
26 Shiga
27 Osaka
28 Nara
29 Mie
30 Wakayama

CHŪGOKU DISTRICT
31 Tottori
32 Okayama
33 Shimane
34 Hiroshima
35 Yamaguchi

SHIKOKU DISTRICT
36 Kagawa
37 Tokushima
38 Ehime
39 Kochi

KYŪSHŪ DISTRICT
40 Fukuoka
41 Saga
42 Nagasaki
43 Kumamoto
44 Oita
45 Miyazaki
46 Kagoshima

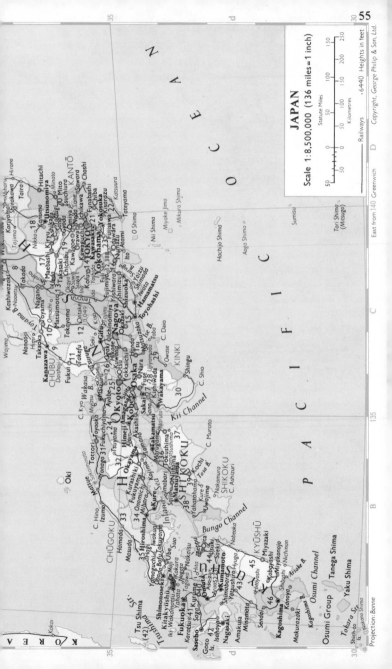

55

JAPAN

Scale 1:8,500,000 (136 miles=1 inch)

Statute Miles
50   0   50   100   150   200   250

Kilometres
50   0   50   100   150   250

Railways ——— ·6440 Heights in feet

Copyright, George Philip & Son, Ltd.

East from 140 Greenwich

Projection: Bonne

PACIFIC OCEAN

KOREA

HONSHU
CHUBU
KANTO
KINKI
CHUGOKU
SHIKOKU
KYUSHU

TOKYO
KYOTO
OSAKA
KOBE
NAGOYA
Yokohama
Kawasaki
Kyushu

Kii Channel
Bungo Channel
Osumi Channel
Tokara Str.

Tanega Shima
Yaku Shima
Osumi Group
Tsu Shima
Goto Is.

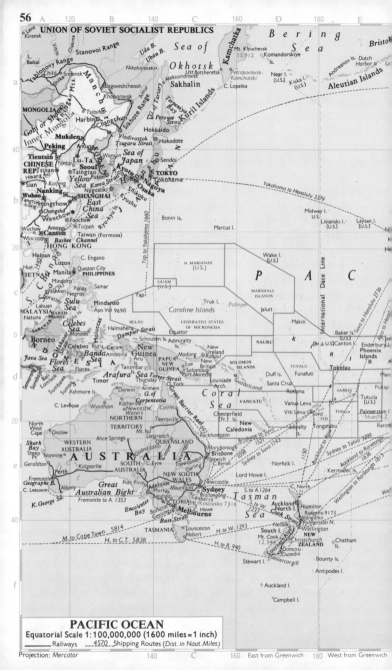

PACIFIC OCEAN
Equatorial Scale 1:100,000,000 (1600 miles=1 inch)

Timor Sea

Bathurst I.
Melville I.
Van Diemen Gulf
Gou

P. Darwin
Darwin
Arnhe

INDIAN

Ashmore I.
C. Londonderry
C. Bougainville
C. Ford
Pt. Blaze
Rum Jungle
Pine Cree
Kather
Daly

OCEAN

York Sound
Buccaneer
Archipelago
King Sound
C. Leveque
Yampi Sound

Wyndham
Mt. Cockburn 1593
Cambridge G.

Victoria
Victoria River Downs
Newcastle Waters
Wave Hill
Woods

Kimberley
Leopold Ras.
Derby
Fitzroy Crossing
Hall's Creek
Dampier Land
C. Baskerville
Broome
C. Bossut
La Grange

Sturt

NORT

TERR

Tennant C

Daver

Larrey Pt. Eighty Mile Beach
P. Hedland
Mount Goldsworthy
Joanna Spring
Reynolds

Dampier Arch.
Dampier
Barrow I.
Onslow
Exmouth Gulf
Fortescue

Cossack
Roebourne
Pilbara
Marble Bar
Nullagine
Wittenoom Gorge

L. Mackay
Macdonn
James Ra

Fortescue
Hamersley Ra.
Mt. Brockman 3654
Mt. Bruce 4024
Ashburton
Ophthalmia Ra.

WESTERN

L. Disappointment

L. Macdonald

Rawlinson Ranges

Hermannsburg
Amadeus
Erl

Pt. Cloates
Learmonth
Barlee Ra.
Mt. Whaleback
Robertson Ra.

Musgrave Ra
Mt. Woodroffe 4970

C. Cuvier
Geographe Channel
Shark B.
Carnarvon
Gascoyne
Mt. Augustus 3627
Gould
Robinson Ras.
2300
Mt. Hale 2400
Peak Hill
Weld Spring
L. Carnegie
Mt. Squires 2270

Dirk Hartog I.
Steep Point
Wooramel
Murchison
Nannine
Big Bell
Cue
Meekatharra
Wiluna

AUSTRALIA

Freycinet L.
Ajana
Northampton
Geraldton
Dongara
Mullewa
Mingenew
Miling
Mt. Magnet
L. Austin
Austin
Sandstone
Lawlers
Mt. Sir Samuel
Leonora
Laverton
Mt. Morgans
Malcolm
Maraling

Yalgoo
L. Barlee
Menzies
Yunndaga
Kalgoorlie-Boulder
Loongana
Deakin
Ooldea
Watson
A

Goomalling
Bonnie Rock
Bencubbin
Coolgardie
Southern Cross
Zanthus
Naretha
Eyre
Eucla
C. Adieu
Thevena
Penong

Gingin
Darling Range
Northam
Merredin
Hyden
Newdegate
Nullarbor Plain

Midland Junc
Perth
Fremantle
York
Quairading
Kellerberrin
The Johnston Lakes
Great Australian Bight

Collie
Pinjarra
Narrogin
Wagin
Pingelly
Pingrup
Ravensthorpe
Esperance
Nuyts Archip

Geographe B
C. Naturaliste
Busselton
Bunbury
Bridgetown
Ongerup
C. Arid
Archipelago of the Recherche
Investi

Augusta
C. Leeuwin
Pemberton
Mt. Barker
Albany

Pt. D'Entrecasteaux
Pt. Nuyts
Denmark
West C. Howe

SOUT

60

SOUTH-EAST AUSTRALIA
Scale 1:8,000,000 (128 miles = 1 inch)

50 · · · · 0 · · · · 50 · · · · 100 Statute Miles
50 · · 0 · · 50 · · 100 · · 150 Kilometres

—— Railways   3060 Heights in feet

Projection: *Bonne*   East from 145°Greenwich

61

A N D

D

150

C

BRISBANE

MORETON

Oakey o Toowoomba Toowong
Binda o Bindle Pittsworth Gatton Wynnum Dunwich Stradbroke I.
Bendena o Moonie Clifton Laidley Rosewood Ipswich Southport
Balonn o St George o Flinton Millmerran Mt. Domville Hendon Boonah Indooroopilly South Coast
o Bollon 2106 Warwick Killarney Kyogle Coolangatta
Nindigully Weir Inglewood Amiens Wilson Beaudesert Murwillumbah
Dirranbandi Thallon Yelarbon Stanthorpe Texas England Ra. Mullumbimby
Goondiwindi 4042 Drake o C.Byron
Dareel o Boomi Mungindi Yetman Deepwater Emmaville Tenterfield Lismore Byron Bay
Angledool Goondubluio Camurra Wariabda Glen Innes Maclean
Collarenebri Moree Inverell Ulmarra
North Central Plain Bellata Tingha NORTHERN Grafton
Walgett Wee Waa Guyra TABLELAND Mt. Hyland Coff's Harbour
Pilliga Narrabri Barraba Armidale Dorrigo Urunya
Coonamble Gwabegar Boggabri Manilla N.WESTN Uralla Bellingen Nambucca Heads
Baradine Coonabara- SLOPE Walcha Macksville
Warren bran Gunnedah Liverpool Plains Werris Cr. Tamworth Hastings Ra. Smithton & Gladstone
Narromine Dubbo Quirindi Liverpool Ra. Murrurundi Kempsey
Wellington Coolah 4500 Scone Wanchope Port Macquarie & Hastings R.
Gulgong Dunedoo Merriwa HUNTER & MANNING Wingham
Mudgee Gloucester Taree Manning
Rylstone Singleton Muswellbrook Forster Tuncurry
CENTRAL Orange Hunter Ra. Kurri Kurri Dungog Sugarloaf Pt.
Cudgegong Newnes Greta Maitland Port Stephens
Bathurst Lithgow Wallsend NEWCASTLE & Port Hunter
TABLE LAND Portland Toronto
Katoomba Gosford
Cowra Penrith Hornsby Broken Bay & Hawkesbury R.
Parramatta Liverpool SYDNEY & Port Jackson
Camden Campbelltown Manly METROPOLITAN
Pictor Cronulla & Botany B.
Wollongong
Goulburn Shellharbour Kiama
CANBERRA Nowra Berry (COMMONWEALTH TERR.)
Queanbeyan Braidwood Jervis Bay
CAP. TER. Batemans Bay
Tumut Moruya
Cooma Narooma
Kosciusko 7316 Nimmitabel
Bega

C
150
D

TASMANIA
On the same scale

Bass Strait
Narracoopa Flinders I.
Currie King I. Furneaux Whitemark
Stokes Pt. Three Hummock Group
Hunter I. Robbins I. C. Barren I.
Smithton Stanley C. Portland
Arthur Wynyard Penguin Scottsdale Herrick
Trowutta Burnie Devonport Bridport
N.W. Ulverstone Sheffield Deloraine Launceston
Waratah Cradle Mt. Mole Cr. Westbury Ben Lomond
5114 Longford St. Marys
Zeehan Mt. Ossa Great Avoca
5309 Lake Campbell Town
C.Sorell W. Tarraleah MID Oatlands Oyster B.
Macquarie Bothwell Apsley Maria I.
Harb. Derwent Brighton SE
Pt Hibbs New Norfolk Bellerive
S. Glenorchy HOBART
Gordon Huonville
Port Davey Geeveston C. Pillar
S.E. Cape Bruny I.
B 145 C

Copyright, George Philip & Son, Ltd.

62

TERRITORY OF PAPUA NEW GUINEA
Scale 1:20,000,000 (320 miles = 1 inch)

PAPUA NEW GUINEA

Vanimo · Aitape · Wewok · Madrika · Sepik · Muller Ra. · Strickland · Fly · Dara · Kikori · Kerema · Delena · Port Moresby · Fo'a/Fo'la · Owen Stanley Ra. · Abau · Buna · Eloa · Tufi · Wau · Morobe · Finschhafen · Lae · Modang · Boroka · Umboi · Karkar I. · Manam · Wasu · Gusap

Schouten Is. · Manus I., Admiralty Is. · Morgenthurg · New Hanover · New Ireland · Bismarck Archipelago · Bismarck Sea · New Britain · Gilau · Gasmata · Rabaul · Buka I. · Kieta · Bougainville · Torokina · Green Is. · Solomon Is.

SOLOMON SEA · Tobriand or Kiriwina Is. · Woodlark I. · D'Entrecasteaux Is. · Normanby I. · Louisiade Arch. · Tagula I. · Samarai

Gulf of Papua · CORAL SEA

QUEENSLAND

C.York · Thursday I. · Prince of Wales I. · Endeavour Str. · P.Musgrave · DuifKen Pt. · Welpon · Cape York · Archer · Peninsula · Holroyd · C.Keerweer · St.Burne Bay · C.Grenville · C.Direction · Princess Charlotte B. · C.Melville · C.Flattery · Cooktown · P.Douglas · Cairns · Mareeba · Atherton · Mt.Mulligan · Mt.Bartle Frere 5287 · Innisfail · Cardwell · Hinchinbrook I. · Ingham · Halifax Bay · C.Cleveland · Townsville · Ayr · Home Hill · Bowen (Pt.Denison) · Proserpine · Repulse B. · Mackay · Broad Sd. · Eton · St.Lawrence · Northumberland Is. · Swain Reefs · C.Townshend · Shoalwater · C.Palmerston · Emu Park · Keppel Bay · Curtis I. · Capricorn Chan. · Rockhampton · Mt.Morgan · Gladstone

C.Arnhem · Caledon Bay · Blue Mud Bay · Groote Eylandt · Limmen Bight · Gulf of Carpentaria · Sir Edward Pellew Group · Vanderlin I. · Wellesley Is. · Mornington · Burketown · Leichhardt · Gregory Ra. · Normanton · Croydon · Georgetown · Einasleigh · Forsayth · Gilbert · Einasleigh · Chillagoe · Lynd · Palmer · Mitchell · Staaten · Laura · Normanby · Mt.Cuthbert · Cloncurry · Mt.Isa · Duchess · Dajarra · Camooweal · Austral Downs · Boulia · Georgina · Diamantina · Burke · Selwyn · Hamilton · Winton · Muttaburra · Aramac · Jericho · Clermont · Blair Athol · Peak Downs · Dysart · Clermont · Emerald · Belyando · L.Galilee · Aramac · Barcaldine · Longreach · Ilfracombe · Isisford · Thomson · Opalton · L.Philippi · Marshall · Hay · Diamantina · Richmond · Hughenden · Prairie · Pentland · Charters Towers · Burdekin · Leichhardt · Bowen · Netherdale · Wessel Is. · Melville · Wessel I's · Maranoa

Wellesley I's · Flinders · Cloncurry · Richmond · Winton · Gregory Ra. · Woolgar · Barkly Tableland

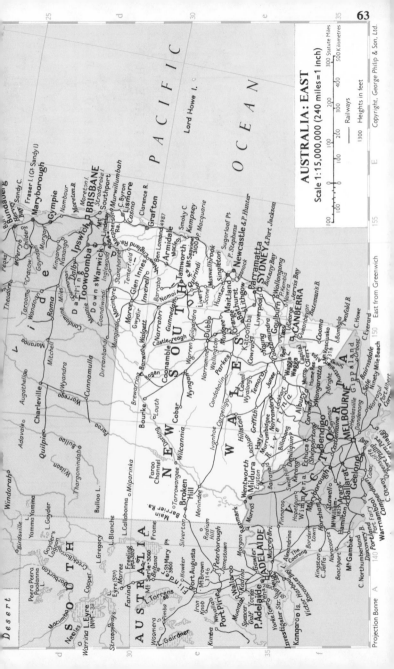

63

AUSTRALIA: EAST

Scale 1:15,000,000 (240 miles=1 inch)

Railways

1300 — Heights in feet

Copyright, George Philip & Son, Ltd.

Projection Bonne

East from Greenwich

PACIFIC

OCEAN

Lord Howe I.

QUEENSLAND

NEW SOUTH WALES

VICTORIA

SOUTH AUSTRALIA

Desert

Brisbane
Ipswich
Toowoomba
Warwick
Maryborough
Gympie
Bundaberg
Fraser I. (Gt. Sandy I.)
Hervey B.
Sandy C.
Nambour
Moreton I.
Stradbroke I.
Southport
Murwillumbah
Lismore
C. Byron
Casino
Grafton
Clarence R.
Roma
Dalby
Miles
Chinchilla
Gayndah
Kingaroy
Nanango
Murgon
Childers
Gin Gin
Mt. Perry
Gladstone

Charleville
Cunnamulla
Augathella
Tambo
Blackall
Adavale
Quilpie
Wyandra
Morven
Mitchell
Amby
Mungallala
Bollon
St. George

Armidale
Tamworth
Glen Innes
Inverell
Tenterfield
Stanthorpe
Moree
Narrabri
Gunnedah
Quirindi
Scone
Muswellbrook
Singleton
Maitland
Newcastle & Pt. Hunter
Port Stephens
Sugarloaf Pt.
C. Hawke
Ben Lomond 4987
Smoky C.
Macksville
Kempsey
Pt. Macquarie
Mt. Seaview 5000

Sydney
Parramatta
Liverpool
Wollongong
Botany Bay
Port Jackson
Katoomba
Lithgow
Bathurst
Orange
Mudgee
Dubbo
Wellington
Parkes
Forbes
Cowra
Young
Cootamundra
Temora
Junee
Wagga Wagga
Gundagai
Yass
Canberra
Goulburn
Nowra
Jervis Bay
Bateman's Bay
Cooma
Bombala
Bega
Eden
C. Howe
Queanbeyan
Mt. Kosciusko 7316

Broken Hill
Wilcannia
Cobar
Bourke
Brewarrina
Walgett
Coonamble
Coonabarabran
Nyngan
Condobolin
Griffith
Hay
Hillston
Ivanhoe
Menindee
Wentworth
Mildura
Euston
Balranald
Deniliquin
Echuca
Shepparton
Swan Hill
Kerang
Bendigo
Castlemaine
Ballarat
Geelong
Melbourne
Seymour
Wangaratta
Benalla
Wodonga
Albury
Corowa
Wagga Wagga
Narrandera
Leeton
Murrumbidgee River
Lachlan R.
Murray R.
Darling R.

Adelaide
Port Adelaide
Gawler
Port Pirie
Port Augusta
Peterborough
Jamestown
Burra
Kadina
Wallaroo
Moonta
Kapunda
Murray Bri.
Morgan
Victor Harbour
Kingscote
Kangaroo Is.
Yorke Pen.
Spencer Gulf
Gulf St. Vincent
Eyre Pen.
Iron Knob
Iron Baron
Whyalla
Woomera
Mt. Serle 3060
Mt. Mary
L. Frome
L. Callabonna
L. Blanche
L. Gregory
Cooper Creek
Cooper's Creek
Strangways
L. Eyre (North) -39
Farina
Marree
Birdsville
Windorah
Yamma Yamma
Goyder's Lagoon
Peera Peera Poolanna L.
Macumba
Naccowlah
Warrina L.
Mt. Babbage

Hamilton
Mt. William 3827
Warrnambool
Portland
C. Northumberland
Mt. Gambier
Millicent
Kingston
Naracoorte
Bordertown
Horsham
Ararat
Stawell
Maryborough
St. Arnaud
Avoca
Pinnaroo
Lameroo
Tailem Bend
The Coorong
Encounter B.
Cape Jaffa
Robe
Beachport

Gippsland
Bairnsdale
Sale
Warragul
Dandenong
Leongatha
Wonthaggi
Ninety Mile Beach
C. Everard
Cann R.
Orbost
Cape Albert
Korumburra

Lord Howe I.

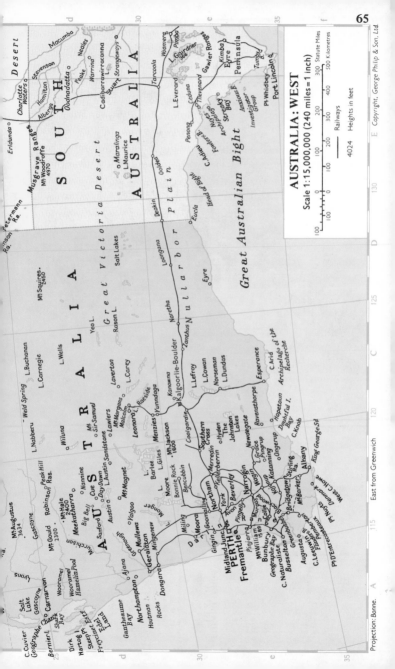

65

AUSTRALIA: WEST

Scale 1:15,000,000 (240 miles = 1 inch)

Railways
4024 ——— Heights in feet

Statute Miles
100   0   100   200   300
Kilometres
100   0   100   200   300   400   500

E *Copyright, George Philip & Son, Ltd*

Projection: Bonne.   East from Greenwich

Charlotte Desert

S O U T H

A U S T R A L I A

Eringa
Macumba
Stevenson
Hamilton
Neales
Peake
Warrina
Cadibarrawirracanna
Stuart Strangeways
Woomera
L. Gairdner
Pimba
Kimba
Gawler Ra.
Eyre
Tumby
Port Lincoln
Eyre Peninsula
Alberga
Oodnadatta
Musgrave Ranges
Mt Woodroffe 4970
Petermann Ra.
Rawlinson Ra.
Mt Squires 2450
Moralinga
L. Maurice
Tarcoola
Kingoonya
Ceduna
Penong
C. Adieu
Nuyts Archipelago
Thevenard
St Francis I.
Streaky Bay
Point Brown
Anxious B.
Investigator Group
Pt Whidbey

Great Victoria Desert

T R A L I A

W E S T E R N

Weld Spring
L. Buchanan
L. Carnegie
L. Nabberu
Wiluna
L. Wells
Yeo L.
Salt Lakes
Rason L.
Noretha
Loongana
Deakin
Eucla
Eyre

Great Australian Bight

Nullarbor Plain

Oodeia
Zanthus
Kanowna
Kalgoorlie-Boulder
L. Lefroy
L. Cowan
Norseman
L. Dundas
Esperance
C. Arid
Archipelago of the Recherche
Ravensthorpe
Hopetoun
Doubtful Bay
C. Knob
King George Sd
West C. Howe
Albany
Denmark
Pt Nuyts
Pt D'Entrecasteaux

L. Carey
Laverton
L. Raeside
Yundaga
Menzies
Mt Morgans
Malcolm
Leonora
Mt Jackson 1600
Southern Cross
Coolgardie
Hyden
The Johnston Lakes
Newdegate
Grace
Pingrup
Ongerup
Gnowangerup
Stirling Ra.
Mt Barker
Bridgetown
Manjimup
C. Leeuwin
Augusta
C. Naturaliste
Geographe Bay
Busselton
Bunbury
Collie
Pinjarra
Mt William 1589

Mt Sir Samuel
Mt Magnet
Cue
Day Dawn
Austin
Sandstone
Big Bell
Nannine
L. Barlee
L. Giles
Merredin
Kellerberrin
Bencubbin
Bonnie Rock
Mukinbudin
Quairading
Bruce Rock
Narembeen
Corrigin
Kondinin
Wagin
Woodanilling
Katanning
Narrogin
Wandering
Brookton
Beverley
York
Northam
Meckering
Goomalling
Dowerin
Wongan Hills
Moora
Gingin
Midland Junction

PERTH
Fremantle

Mt Jackson
Yalgoo
Mongers
L. Moore
Milling
Dalwallinu

Mt Sanford
Mingenew
Dongara
Geraldton
Northampton
Ajana
Mullewa
Greenough
Houtman Rocks

Salt Lake
C. Cuvier
Geographe Chan.
Bernier I.
Dirk Hartog
Steep Pt.
Freycinet Estn.
Gantheaume Bay
Shark Bay
Hamelin Pool
Woorame
Carnarvon
Gascoyne
Mt Gould 2300
Mt Hale 2400
Robinson Ra.
Peak Hill Ras.
Meekatharra
Murchison
Mt Augustus 3634
Lyons
Yinnietharra

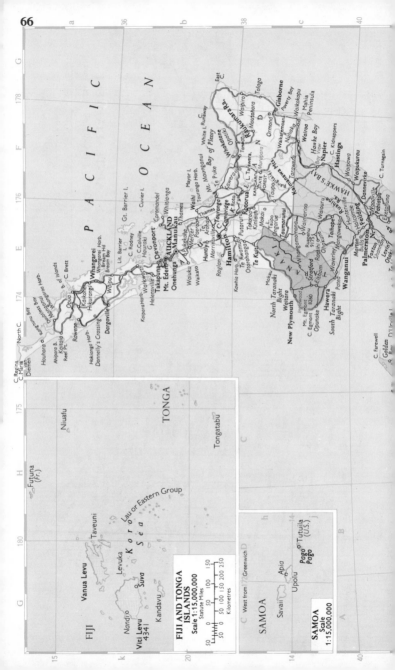

G

a 36 b 38 c 40

178 F 176 E 174

P A C I F I C   O C E A N

C. Regina
Maria
van Diemen
North C.
Cape Regina

Houhora
Ahipara B.
Kaitaia
Reef Pt.

Sandy's Bay
Spirits Bay
North Cape

Ahipara Hbr.
Whangarei Hbr.
Bream Bd.
Bream Bay

Opua
Kaikohe
Hokianga
Hokianga Hbr.
Rawene
Donnelly's Crossing
Dargaville
Waipu

Kaipara Hbr.
Helensville
Wellsford
Warkworth

Bay of Islands
C. Brett
Lit. Barrier
C. Rodney

Gt. Barrier I.
C. Colville
Houraki
Cuvier I.
Coromandel
Mercury Bd.

Takapuna
Devonport
AUCKLAND
Mt. Eden
Onehunga
Manukau
Manukau Hbr.
Thames
Whitianga

Mayor I.
Mt. Moehau
Te Puke
Tauranga
Waihi
Tauranga

Waiuku
Waikato
Wai
Pukekohe
Paeroa
Morrinsville
Huntly
Ngaruawahia
Hamilton
Cambridge
Te Awamutu
Matamata
Putaruru
Rotorua
L. Rotorua
L. Taupo
Tokoroa
Te Kuiti
Mokau
Ongarue
Taumarunui
Waiouru

East C.
Tologa
Gisborne
RAUKUMARA Ra.
White I. Runaway
C. Runaway
Waiapu
Opotiki
Whakatane
Opotoki

Poverty Bay
Wairoa

Mahia
Peninsula
Waikokopu
Mohaka
Mt. Ruapehu
9175
Napier
Hastings
Hawke Bay
C. Kidnappers
Waipukurau
Woodville
Dannevirke
C. Turnagain

Raglan
Kawhia Hbr.
North Taranaki
Bight
New Plymouth
Waitara
Mt. Egmont
Opunake
C. Egmont
8260
Inglewood
Stratford
Eltham
Hawera
South Taranaki
Bight
Patea
Waverley
Waitotara
Waiouru
Wanganui
Bulls
Marton
Halcombe
Feilding
Palmerston N.
Shannon
Levin
Otaki

C. Farewell
Golden
Bay

H 175 C 180 G

TONGA

Niuatu
Futuna
(Fr.)

Taveuni
Vanua Levu
Levuka
Lau or Eastern Group

FIJI
Nandi
Viti Levu
4341
Suva
Kandavu

Tongatabu

Koro Sea

**FIJI AND TONGA
ISLANDS**
Scale 1:15,000,000

Statute Miles
50 0 50 100 150 200 250
0 50 100 150 200
Kilometres

C West from 72° Greenwich D h

SAMOA

Savaii
Apia
Upolu
Pago Pago
Tutuila
(U.S.)

SAMOA
1:15,000,000

14

A 40

15 20
k j

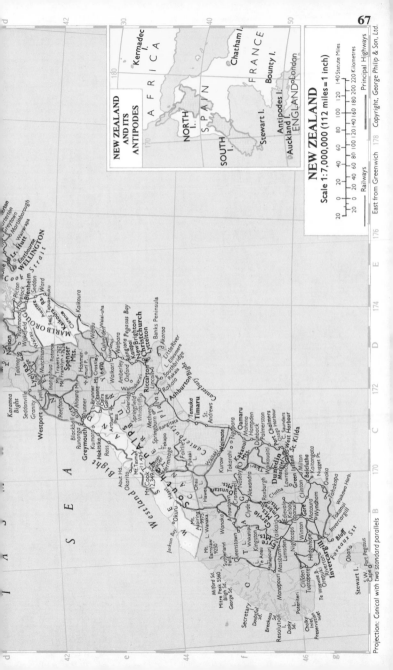

67

NEW ZEALAND
AND ITS
ANTIPODES

Kermadec I.

AFRICA

NORTH

SOUTH
I.

SPAIN

FRANCE

Chatham I.

Bounty I.

Stewart I.

Antipodes I.

Auckland I.

ENGLAND London

NEW ZEALAND

Scale 1:7,000,000 (112 miles=1 inch)

20 0 20 40 60 80 100 120 140 Statute Miles

20 0 20 40 60 80 100 120 140 160 180 200 220 Kilometres

—— Railways —— Principal Highways

East from Greenwich

176 178 Copyright, George Philip & Son, Ltd.

Projection: Conical with two standard parallels

North (place names, partial)

Castlepoint
Greytown
Carterton
Martinborough

Mt. Hutt
WELLINGTON
Eastbourne
Masterton
Wairarapa

Cook Strait

Palliser C.

E. Nelson
Picton
Blenheim
Seddon
Ward

Richmond
Redmond
Kaikoura

Riwaka
Motueka
Waimea
Tadmor

MARLBOROUGH

Mt. Tapuaenuku

Karamea Bight

Seddonville
Granity

Westport

Inangahua
Reefton
Murchison
Lyell

Spenser Mts.

Mt. Crossley
Hanmer
Hope
Amuri P.

Waiau-uha
Waiau

Mt. Travers 7,674
Mt. Franklin 7,674

Mt. Crossley

Blackball
Runanga
Brunner
Kumara
Otira
Gorge

TASMAN SEA

Mt. 6,670
L.

Culverden
Oxford
Amberley
Rangiora

Waiau
Waikari

Hurunui

Arahura Pass
Kumara
Ross

Greymouth
Hokitika

Otira
Arthur's Pass

Lake Brunner
L.
Coleridge

Springfield
Windwhistle
Lincoln
Riccarton

Pegasus Bay
New Brighton
CHRISTCHURCH
Lyttelton

Banks Peninsula
Akaroa

Abut Hd.
Okarito

Mt. Tasman 11,475
Mt. Cook 12,349

Methven

L. Tekapo
Rakaia
Rangitata
Fairlie

Little River
L. Ellesmere
Southbridge
Rakaia

Ashburton

SOUTHERN ALPS

Canterbury Plains

St. Andrews
Pukaki
Temuka
Timaru

Westland Bight

Jackson Bay
Okuru

Mt. Aspiring 9,957

L. Wanaka
L. Hawea
Hawea
Pukaki
L. Pukaki

Burke's Pass
Fairlie

Ngapara
Kurow
Naseby
Oamaru
Moeraki
Hampden

Waitaki

Mt. Earnslaw 9,250

Wakatipu
Queenstown
L. Wanaka
Arrowtown
Cardrona
Cromwell
Clyde
Alexandra

St. Bathans
Ranfurly
Palmerston
Moeraki
Dunback

Waikouaiti
C. Saunders
Port Chalmers
Mosgiel
DUNEDIN
West Harbour
St. Kilda

Milford Sd.
Mitre Peak 5,560
Bligh Sd.
George Sd.

Te Anau
L. Te Anau
Manapouri
L. Manapouri

Garvie Mts.

Kingston
Lumsden
Kelso

Roxburgh
Beaumont

Tuapeka
Lawrence
Milton
Waihola

Balclutha
Owaka
Romahapa
Kaitangata
Green Island

Nugget Pt.

Secretary I.
Doubtful Sd.
Resolution I.
Dusky Sd.
Breaksea Sd.

Manapouri

Mossburn
Wakapatu
Otautau

Winton
Wyndham
Mataura
Gore

Mataura
Edendale
Wyndham

Tokanui
Waikawa Harb.

Chalky Inlet
Preservation Inlet

L. Poteriteri

Clifden
Tuatapere
Orepuki

Riverton
Wallacetown
INVERCARGILL

Waimatuku
Makarewa
Greenpoint
Nightcaps
Hedgehope

Foveaux Strait

Bluff

Oban
Port Pegasus

Stewart I.

S.W. Cape
Port Pegasus

42 44 46 42 44 46

170 172 174 176 178

B C D E

b c d e f g

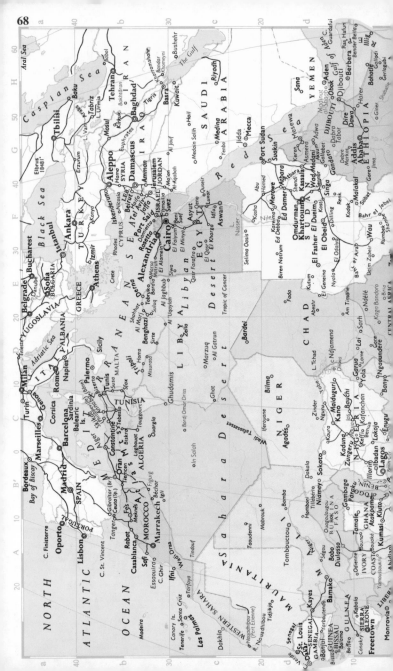

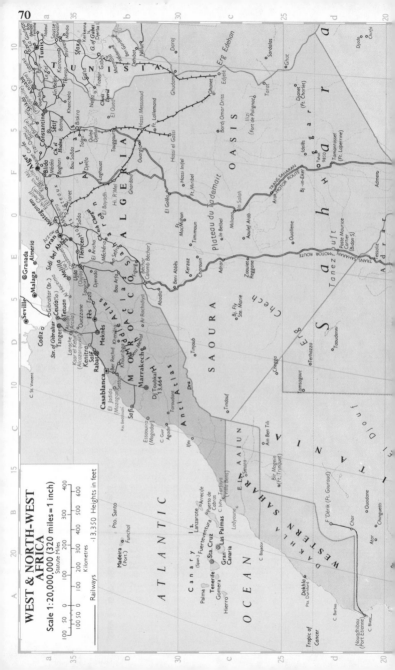

70

WEST & NORTH-WEST AFRICA

Scale 1:20,000,000 (320 miles=1 inch)

Statute Miles
100 50 0   100   200   300   400
Kilometres
100 50 0   100   200   300   400   500   600

·13,350 Heights in feet

Railways

TUNISIA

Tunis · Hammamet · Nabeul
Sousse · Monastir
Kairouan
Sfax
G. of Gabes · Djerba

Constantine
Sétif · Ch. el Hadna
Batna · Biskra
Khenchela
El Oued

ALGERIA

ATLAS
Blida · Médéa
Boghari · Bou Saâda
Djelfa
Laghouat

Oran · Sidi bel Abbès · Tlemcen
Mostaganem
Mascara
Saïda
El Aricha · Aïn Sefra · Géryville
Méchéria · Figuig · R'Kel
El Goléa
Colomb Béchar · Beni Abbès

Ghardaïa
Touggourt · Ouargla
Hassi Messaoud
Bordj Omar Driss
Edjelé
Ghudames

OASIS
Hassi el Gassi
Hassi Inifel
Ft. Miribel
In Salah · Ft. Mac-Mahon
In Belbel
Aoulef Arab · Reggane
Zaouiet · Adrar
Timmoun

Erg Edehen

Ahaggar
In Ecker · Idelès
Tamanrasset (Ft. Laperrine)
Djanet (Ft. Charlet)
Tarat
Sardalas
Ghat

TRANS-SAHARAN MOTOR ROUTE

Bir-in-Eker
Admer
In Azaoua
Agades

MOROCCO
Tanger · Ceuta (Sp.) · Tetouan
Gibraltar (Br.) · Melilla (Sp.)
Larache · Ksar el Kebir · Arcila
Meknès · Fès · Taza · Oujda
Rabat · Kenitra
Casablanca
Safi
Essaouira (Mogador) · Agadir
Marrakech
Dj. Toubkal 13,664

High Atlas · Anti Atlas
Draa

SAOURA
Beni Abbès · Abadla · Tindouf
Tinduf

SEGUIET EL HAMRA
Tabelbala

ATLANTIC

C. St. Vincent
Seville · Granada · Almería
Cádiz · Málaga
Gibraltar
Str. of Gibraltar

Madeira (Port.)
Funchal · Pto. Santo

Canary Is. (Span.)
Lanzarote · Arrecife
Fuerteventura
Palma · Tenerife · Gran Canaria · Las Palmas
Gomera · Sta. Cruz · Puerto de Cabras
Hierro

C. Juby · Tarfaya (Villa Bens)

WESTERN SAHARA
Ifni
Cap Bojador
Bir Moghrein (Ft. Trinquet)
Aïn Ben Tili

DAKHLA (Port. Etienne)
C. Barbas
Nouadhibou (Port Etienne)
C. Blanc

MAURITANIA
F'Dérik (Ft. Gouraud)
Chegga
Atar · Ouadane
Chinguetti

EL DJOUF

OCEAN

Tropic of Cancer

El Aaiún

SAHARA

Tanezrouft

Erg Chech

ADRAR
Poste Maurice Cortier (Bidon 5)
Poste Weygand
Ain Salah

Plateau du Tademaït
Ft. Mackenzie
Miliana · In Salah
Ouallene

Bir Fly (Ste. Marie)
Cheggo
Taoudenni
Tamsagourt

Timiaouine · Kerzaz
Cragnou
Dreoub · Ait Rachidya

Tinguit · Tizi
Ouaouizeght · Beni Mellal
Kasba Tadla · Khouribga
Midelt · Rich
Ksar es Souk (Alcazarquivir)
El Jadida (Mazagan)

OCEAN

·13,350

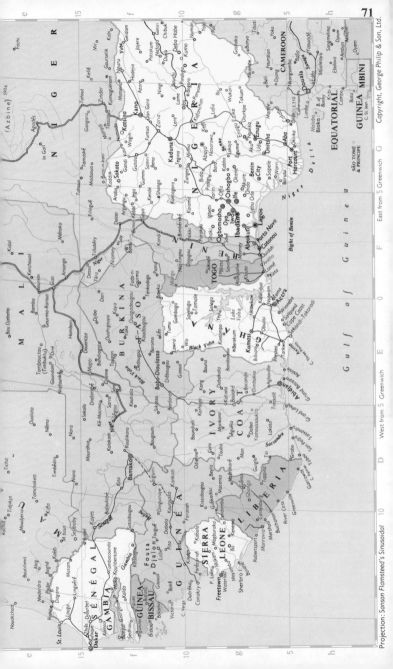

71

Projection: Sanson Flamsteed's Sinusoidal

Copyright, George Philip & Son, Ltd.

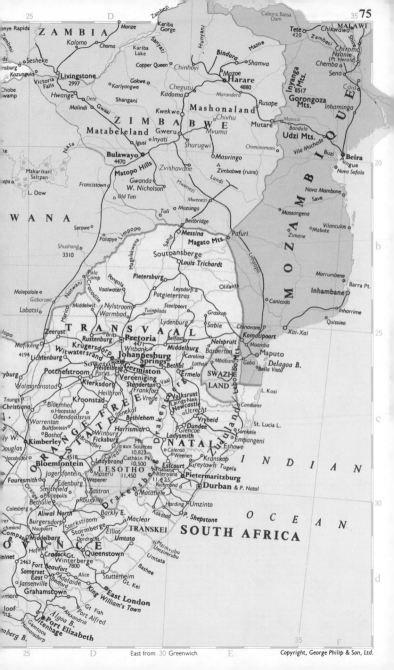

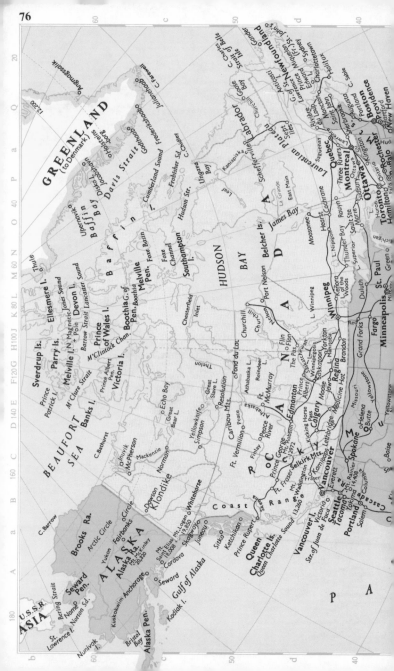

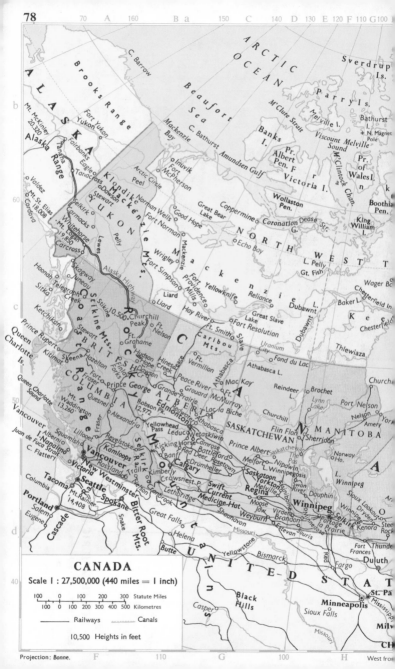

CANADA

Scale 1 : 27,500,000 (440 miles = 1 inch)

| 100 | 0 | 100 | 200 | 300 | Statute Miles |
| 100 | 0 | 100 | 200 | 300 | 400 | 500 | Kilometres |

—————— Railways   ~~~~~~~ Canals

10,500 Heights in feet

Projection: *Bonne.*

78

ARCTIC OCEAN

Sverdrup Is.

C. Barrow

Beaufort Sea

Parry Is.

Brooks Range

Bathurst I.
+ N. Magnet Pole

ALASKA

C. Bathurst

M'Clure Strait

Melville I.

Viscount Melville Sound

Mt. McKinley 20,320

Fort Yukon

Yukon

Alaska Range

Fairbanks

Eagle

Tanacross

Mackenzie Bay

Banks I.

Pr. Albert Pen. F

M'Clintock Chan.

Pr. of Wales I.

k

Valdez
Mt. St. Elias 18,008
Cordova

Inuvik
Fort McPherson

Victoria I.

Arctic Circle

Peel

60

Boothia Pen.

Skagway
Carmacks
Whitehorse
Mt. Logan 19,850
Carcross

YUKON

Norman Wells
Good Hope
Fort Norman

Coppermine

Wollaston Pen.

Coronation G.

Dease Str.

King William I.

Hoonah
Juneau
Telegraph Creek
Sitka
Stikine Mts.
Peak 10,500

Wrigley
Fort Simpson

Great Bear Lake

Echo Bay

L. Pelly

NORTH WEST

Wager B

Ketchikan
Prince Rupert

Liard
Liard

Fort Yellowknife
Providence
Mills

Reliance

Gt. Fish

Baker L

Chesterfield In

Chesterfie

Queen Charlotte Is.

Ft. Grahame
Ft. Nelson

Hay River
Ft. Smith
Great Slave Lake

Dubawnt L.

K e e

Queen Charlotte Sound

Kitimat
Skeena
Hazelton

Hudson Hope
Hinea
Finlay

Ft. Vermilion

Uranium

Fond du Lac

Dubawnt

Thlewiaza

Vancouver I.
Alberni
Nanaimo

BRITISH COLUMBIA

Caribou Mts.

Fort Resolution

Athabasca L.

Churc

Waddington 13,260

Peace River
Grande Prairie
Grouard
Ft. McMurray

Reindeer L.

Brochet

Port Nelson

Robson Pk. 12,972

Quesnel
Alexandria
Fraser
Prince George

Edmonton
Lac la Biche
Athabasca

Flin Flon

Lynn Lake

Nelson

Yor

Lillooet
Squamish
Revelstoke
Yellowhead Pass

Leduc
Wetaskiwin

Prince Albert

SASKATCHEWAN

Churchill

Sherridon

Amery

50

Vancouver
New Westminster
Victoria
Kamloops
Kicking Horse
Banff
Camrose
Red Deer
Rosetown

Battleford
North

Melfort
Nipawin

The Pas

MANITOBA

N

Seattle
Tacoma
Mt. Rainier 14,408

Kimberly
Crowsnest P.
Nelson
Trail
Rossland

Calgary
Drumheller
Saskatoon
Winnipegosis

Norway Ho.

L. Winnipeg

Dauphin

Portland
Salem
Eugene

Cascade

Columbia

Bitter Root Mts.

Spokane

Lethbridge
Cranbrook

Medicine Hat
Swift Current

Regina
Moose Jaw

York
Melville

Swan

Portage la Prairie

Sioux Lookout

Kenora

Stock

Great Falls

Helena
Butte

Snake

Shaunavon

Weyburn
Virden
Brandon
Souris
Estevan

Winnipeg

Selkirk

Dry

d

Missouri

Yellowstone

UNITED

Bismarck

Red

Fort Frances

Thunde

Duluth

40

Casper

Black Hills

Sioux Falls

STAT

Fargo

Minneapolis

Mississippi

St. Pa

Mil

CH

Caspe

Missouri

Juan de Fuca Strait
C. Flattery

West fro

F 110 G 100 H

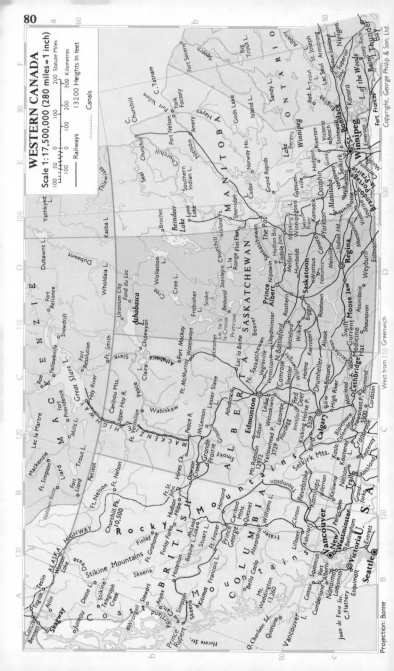

80

WESTERN CANADA

Scale 1:17,500,000 (280 miles = 1 inch)

13200 Heights in feet

Railways

Canals

Copyright, George Philip & Son, Ltd.

West from 110 Greenwich

Projection: Bonne

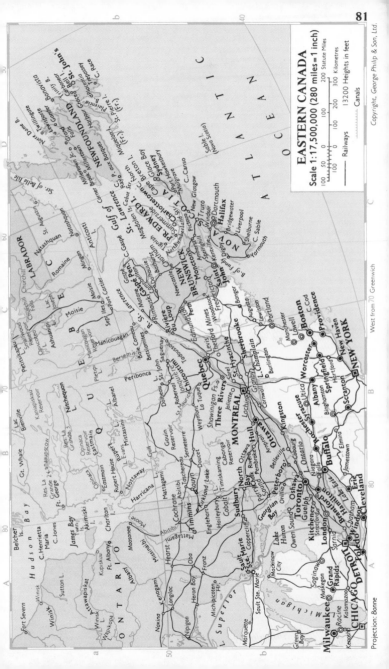

82

A 130 120 a B 110 C 100

CANADA (C A N ... N)

Saskatoon
Kamloops
Calgary
Vancouver Is.
Nanaimo
Vancouver
Bellingham
Crows Nest Pass
Moose Jaw
S. Saskatchewan
Regina
Juan de Fuca Str.
C. Flattery
Victoria
Trail
Lethbridge
Medicine Hat
Brandon
Everett
Seattle
Spokane
Havre
Milk
Glasgow
Buford
Minot
L. Manit.
Tacoma
Mt. Rainier 14,408
N. Yakima
WASHINGTON
Missouri
Dickinson
N. DAK.
Astoria
Portland
Oregon City
Salem
Corvallis
Eugene
Columbia
Walla Walla
MONTANA
Helena
Great Falls
Missouri
Miles City
Bismarck
Grangeville
Baker
Butte
Bozeman
Red Lodge
Billings
Hardin
Sheridan
Yellowstone
OREGON
Weiser
IDAHO
Boise
Rexburg
Lead
S. DAK.
Cham...
C. Blanco
Medford
Klamath Falls
Silver City
Shoshone
Idaho Falls
Pocatello
Yellowstone National Park
Gannett Pk. 13,785
WYOMING
Black Hills
Rapid City
C. Mendocino
Eureka
Mt. Shasta 14,162
Gt. Salt Lake
Logan
Evanston
Rock Spring
Casper
Crawford
Mullen
NEBRA
40
Winnemucca
Elko
Ogden
Salt Lake City
Laramie
Cheyenne
Long's Pk. 14,255
N. Platte
McCook
Reno
Carson City
Tonopah
NEVADA
Great Basin
UTAH
Richfield
Rawlins
Front Range
Boulder
Denver
COLORADO
Golden Gate
Sacramento
San Francisco
Oakland
San Jose
Fresno
Mt. Whitney 14,495
Death Valley -276
Las Vegas
Wasatch
Grand Canyon
Colorado Plat.
Farmington
Pikes Pk. 14,109
Colorado Springs
Pueblo
Durango
Blanca Pk. 14,317
Dodge City
KA...
Bakersfield
Mojave Desert
Salton Sea
Colorado
Gallup
Santa Fe
Dalhart
Amarillo
Oklah...
Los Angeles
Long Beach
Riverside
ARIZONA
Phoenix
Flagstaff
Winslow
Albuquerque
NEW MEXICO
Llano
Childress
Wichita
Lubbock
San Diego
Mexicali
Yuma
Gila
Tucson
Silver City
Deming
Bisbee
Ciudad Juárez
El Paso
Roswell
Estacado
Carlsbad
Pecos
Sweet Water
S Angelo
Fo...
PACIFIC OCEAN
120
MEXICO

ALASKA
Scale 1 : 25,000,000
50   0   50 100 150 200 Miles
50   0 100 200 300 Km.

Barrow
Point Barrow
Wainwright
Harrison Bay
Prudhoe Bay
Colville
Inuvik
C. Lisburne
Pt. Hope
Noatak
Baird Mts.
Brooks Range
Chandalar
Porcupine
YUKON
East Cape
Pt. of Wales
Bering Strait
Kotzebue
Shungnak
Arctic Circle
Bettles
Beaver
Fort Yukon
Peel
Seward Pen.
Shelton
Candle
Koyukuk
Hughes
Yukon
Rampart
Circle
Eagle
Nome
Solomon
Council
Nulato
Tanana
Hot Springs
Nenana
Ruby
Fairbanks
Dawson
Kwiguk
Kaltag
Ruby
Mt. Hayes 13,740
Tanana
St. Lawrence (U.S.)
Norton Sound
Unalakleet
Ophir
Mt. McKinley 20,320
Talkeetna
16,208 Mt. Blackburn
Kluane
Whitehorse
C. Romanzof
Kotlik
Anvik
Holy Cross
Alaska Range
Palmer
Center
Copper
Wrangell Mts.
Mt. Logan 19,850
White Pass
Nunivak I.
Kuskokwim
Matanuska
Anchorage
Valdez
Cordova
Kennecott
Mt. St. Elias 18,008
Skagway
Bethel
Kendio
Whittier
Latouche
Montague I.
Yakutat
Mt. Fairweather 15,320
Juneau
Admiralty
Kuskokwim Bay
Iliamna Mt. 10,116
Iliamna Lake
Seldovia
Seward
Homer
Chichagof I.
Sitka
Petersburg
Wrangell
C. Newenham
Nushagak
Katmai Vol. 7000
Cook
GULF OF ALASKA
Baranof I.
Alexander Archipelago
Prince of Wales I.
Ketchikan
Ru...
Bristol Bay
C. Newenham
Ugashik Lakes
Afognak I.
Kodiak
Karluk
Kodiak I.
Trinity Is.
Dall I.
Dixon Entrance
Prin...
Port Moller
Alaska Peninsula
Graham I.
Skeena
Stikine
Unimak I.
Sanak I.
Unimak Passage
Chirikof I.
Shumagin Is.
Queen Charlotte Is.
Mor...

Hawaii inset:
160
Mana
Kauai
Lehua
Waimea
Niihau
Kaula
Kauai Ch...
Wai...
Pearl...

60
BERING SEA

Projection: Conical.   160   C   West from 150 Greenwich   D   140   E

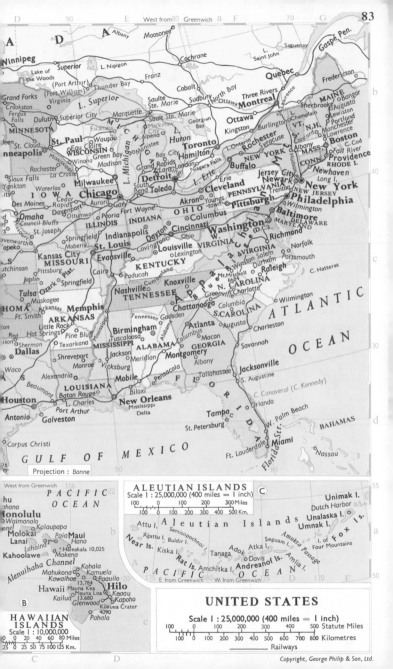

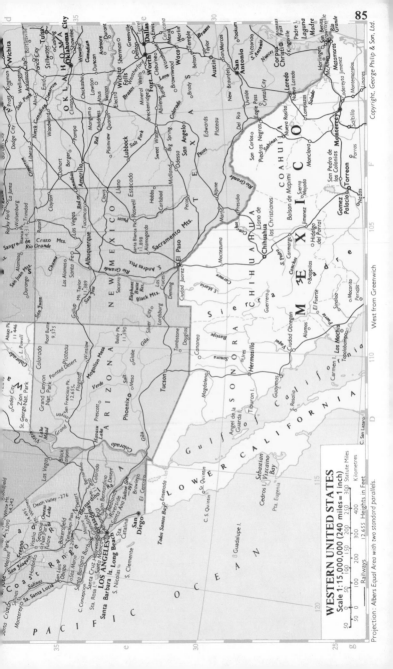

85

WESTERN UNITED STATES
Scale 1:15,000,000 (240 miles=1 inch)

Railways   12,655 Heights in Feet

Projection: Albers Equal Area with two standard parallels.

Copyright, George Philip & Son, Ltd.

West from Greenwich

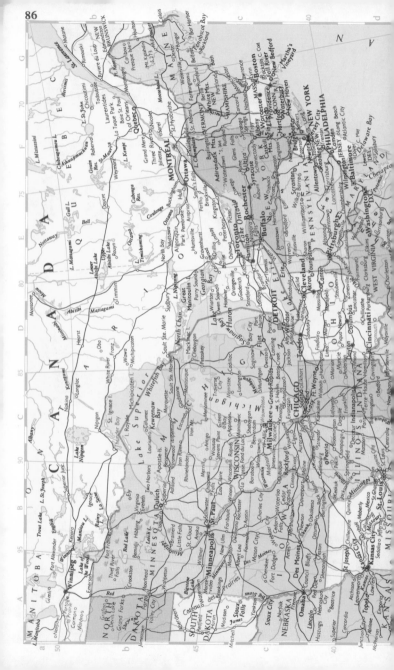

87

EASTERN UNITED STATES

Scale 1:15,000,000 (240 miles=1 inch)

Kilometres
Statute Miles

12,655   Heights in feet

Railways

Projection: Albers Equal Area with two standard parallels

Copyright, George Philip & Son, Ltd.

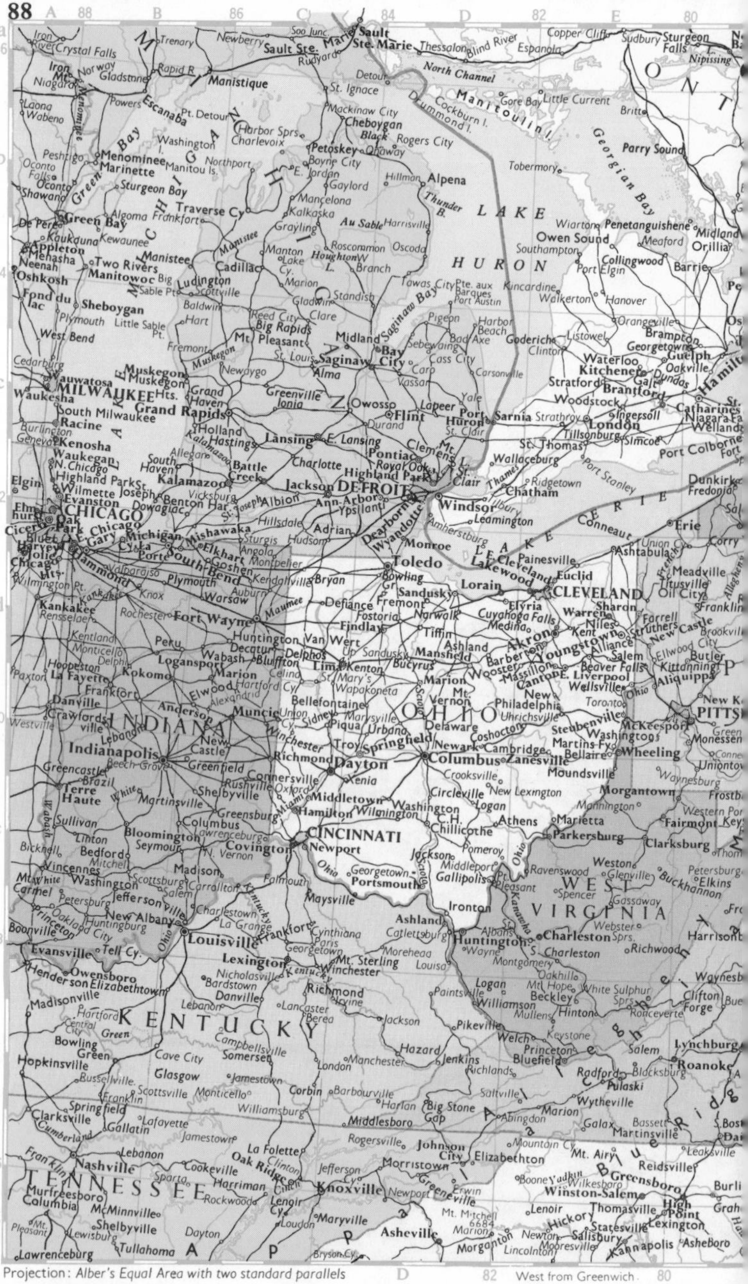

MICHIGAN

LAKE HURON

LAKE ERIE

OHIO

INDIANA

KENTUCKY

TENNESSEE

WEST VIRGINIA

ONTARIO

Georgian Bay

Green Bay

MILWAUKEE
CHICAGO
DETROIT
CLEVELAND
CINCINNATI
Indianapolis
Columbus
Louisville
Lexington
Nashville
Knoxville
Toledo
Fort Wayne
Dayton
Akron
Youngstown
PITTS(burgh)

Sault Ste. Marie
Green Bay
Oshkosh
Sheboygan
Racine
Kenosha
Grand Rapids
Lansing
Flint
Saginaw
Bay City
Kalamazoo
Evansville

Sarnia
London
Windsor

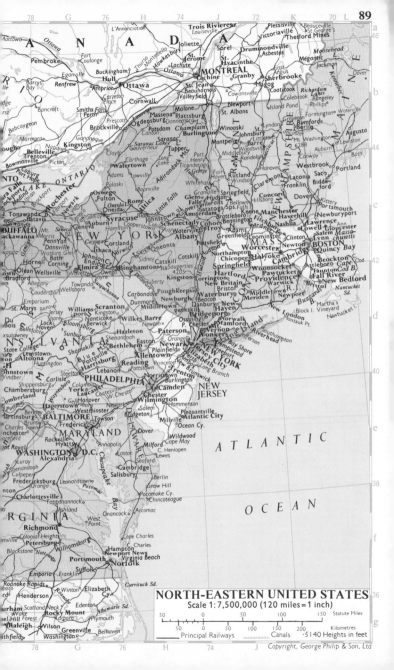

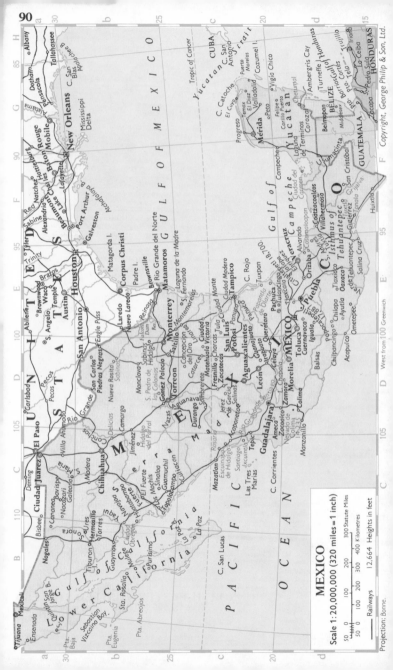

MEXICO

Scale 1:20,000,000 (320 miles = 1 inch)

50 0   100   200   300 Statute Miles

50 0   100   200   300   400 Kilometres

— Railways   12,664 Heights in feet

Projection: Bonne.

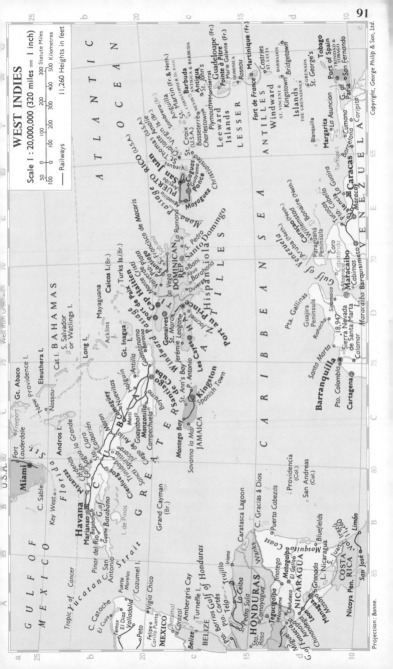

91

WEST INDIES

Scale 1 : 20,000,000 (320 miles = 1 inch)

Statute Miles
50 0 100 200 300 Statute Miles

0 100 200 300 400 500 Kilometres

— Railways

11,260 Heights in feet

Copyright, George Philip & Son, Ltd.

Projection: Bonne.

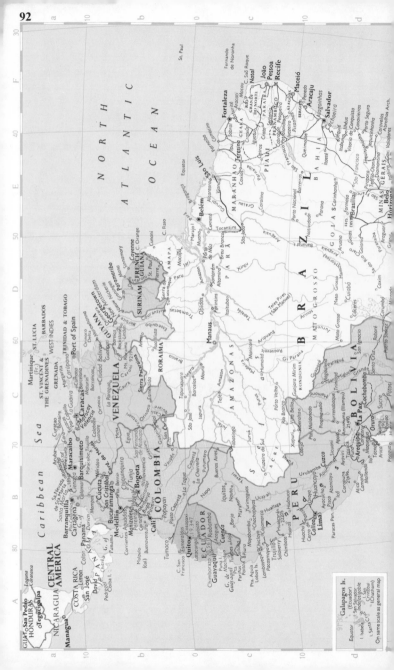

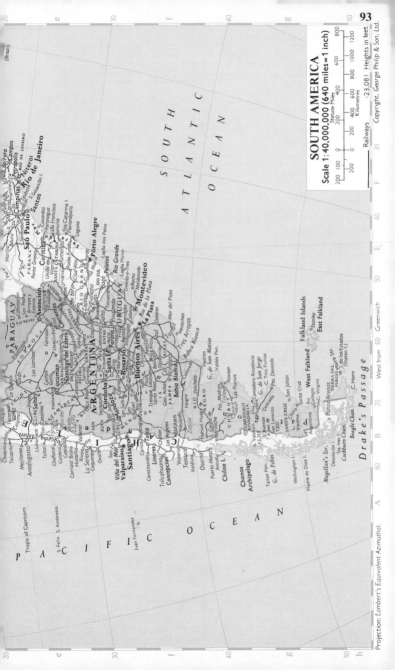

70   B   65   C   60   D

ACRE

Caracol   Caritianas   Sta. Cruz   Theodore Roosevelt   Sierra dos Api

Rio Branco   Abuná   Abuná   Ariquemes

Xapurio   Villa Bella   Vila Murtinho   RONDÔNIA   Presidente Hermes

Taai   Brasiléia   Sta. Rosa   Guajará-Mirim   Ser   Pimenta Bueno

Inapari   Cobija   Orton   Riberalta   Bargo de   Melgaça

Piedras   Manchester   Madre de Dios   Príncipe da Beira   Vilhena   Juruena

Manu   Pto. Maldonado   Madidi   Santo Antonio   Utiariti

Cord. de Mocusani   Ixiamas   L.Rogoaguado   Itonamas   Guaporé   MAT

Sandia   Exaltación   Baures   precis

Caravaya   Sta. Ana   L.Rogagua   Magdalena

Nev.de Vilcanota   Apolo   Rurrenabaque   Baures   La Esperanza   Huanchaca   MataGrosso

Ayavi   Asángaro   Huancane   San Borja   Trinidad   San Martin   Cuia

Juliaca   Lampa   Lake Titicaca   Blanco   Ascención   Sta. Bárbara   Sto. Anto

Puno   Juli   Ancohuma (Illampú)   Coroico   Mamoré   Concepción   Sta. Bárbara   Cáceres

Omate   Guaqui   La Paz   Illimani   Inquisivi   Grande   San Ignacio   San Matias   Cuiab

Laillahue   Viacha   Corocoro   Eucaliptus   El Cerro   San Miguel   Petas

Moquegua   Torata   Guaqui   Desaguadero   Cochabamba   Portachuelo   L. Concepción   Puerto Quijarro

Tacna   Charaña   BOLIVIA   Cord. di Cochabamba   Santa Cruz   San José   Sto. Corazón

Arica   Sajama   Corque   Oruro   Vila Vila   Motacucito   San Juan   Robore   Tucabaca

Negrillos   L. Poopó   Uncía   Grande   Cabezas   Corumb

Pisagua   Sillahuay   Challapata   Sucre   Yati   Puerto Suarez   Porto Esp

Caleta Buena   Sal. de Coipasa   Rio Mulatos   Charagua   Paraguá   Ft. Ayacucho   Forte Coimbra

Iquique   Pozo Almonte   Potosí   San Lucas   Camiri   Bahia Negra   Salinas de Guaramocas

Pintados   Pica   Salar de Uyuni   Cuzco   Huanchaca   Cuevo   Olimpo

Lagunas   Uyuni   Pulacayo   Cotogaita   Barranco Branco

Collahuasi   Ollogue   Chiguana   Atocha   Pilaya   Villa Montes   Ft. Siracuas   Porto Murtinl

Loa   Quillagua   Tupiza   Tarija   Ft. D'Orbigny   Corrales   Minas-cué   Pto. Sastre   Bela Vista

Tocopilla   Toco   Tocarpuri   Villazón   Yacuiba   Pto. Casado   Apa. Pedro

Chuquicamata   Sierra Gorda   Licancaour   Rinconada   Aguaray   Chaco   Boreal   Pto. Pinasco   Cabc

Pta. Angamos   Salar de Atacama   Humahuaca   Iturbe   Tartagal   Ft. Guachalla   PARAGUAY

Mejillones   Susques   Embarcación   El Chorro   Ft. Gen. Diaz   Concepción   Horc

Pta. Tetas   S. Antonio de los Cobres   Orán   Los Blancos   Chaco   Central   San

Caleta Coloso   Ledesma   Chañaral   El Pintado   Confuso

Rosario   Aguas Blancas   Rivadavia   Las Lomitas   Rosari

Achinal   Jujuy   Florencio   Villa Haye

Taltal   Antofagasta de la Sierra   Perico   Salta   Güemes   Joaquín V. González   Asunción   Ypacara

Sta. Catalina   Alemania   Taco Pozo   Pirané   Parag

Chañaral   Leon Muerto   Rosario de la Frontera   Ft. Lavalle   Carapeguá   Borja

Potrerillos   Metán   San José del Boquerón   Rio Muerto   Formosa   V

Los Pozos   Pueblo Hundido   Trancas   Campo Gallo   El Zappallar   Pres. R. S. Peña   Pilar   Ignacio

Caldera   Inca de Oro   San Francisco   Sta. Maria   Burruyacú   Las Cejas   Alhuampa   Avid Terai

Copiapó   Ojos del Salado   Tucumán   Aguilares   Hondo   V. Angelo   Resistencia   S. Luis   Gen. Paz

Tres Puentes   Andalgalá   Albardi   La Cocha   La Banda   P. Pineda   Charadai   Corrientes   Apostol

Punta de Diaz   Carrizal Bajo   Tinogasta   Frías   Santiago del Estero   Quimili   Barranqueras   Empedrado   Sto. Tomé

Huasco   Yerba Buena   Catamarca   Añatuya   Las Toscas   Bella Vista

Vallenar   Mazán   Chumbicha   Tostado   Los Juries   Intiyaco   Reconquista   Pedro R. Fernandez   Alvear

La Serena   Co. del Toro   Famatina   La Rioja   Chilecito   Ceballos   Quebrachos   Selva   Vera   Goya   Mercedes   Curuzú   Cuatiá

Coquimbo   Guandacol   Recreo   Villa   (Rio Seco)   Ceres   S. Cristobal   Esquina   Mte.   Caseros   Urugu

Tongoy   Vicuña   Jáchal   Patquia   Sta. Maria   Los Rubios   Javier   La Paz   Artigas   Quaraí

Ovalle   Iglesia   Gob. Gordillo   Sabines   Morteros   S. Justo   Concordia   Cabellos   Salto

Castaño   Colingasta   Serrezuela   Dean Funes   Chaquita   Rafaela   Esperanza   Nare   Federacion

Illapel   Albardón   Chepes   Las Cerrillos   Santa Fé   Paysandú

Los Vilosos   Salamanca   San Juan   Independencia   Córdoba   S. Francisco   Paraná   Tacuarembó

Papudo   Quillota   San Felipe   Carizal Honda   Alta Gracia   Los Varillas   Diamante   Villaguay

Viña del Mar   Andes   Aconcagua   Ovalle   Quines   Sta. Rosa   Villa Maria   Bell Ville   Las Rosas   Concepción   del Urug.   URU

Mendoza   S. Francisco   Cañada de Gomez   Rosario   Gualeguay

Cruz Alta   Chucul

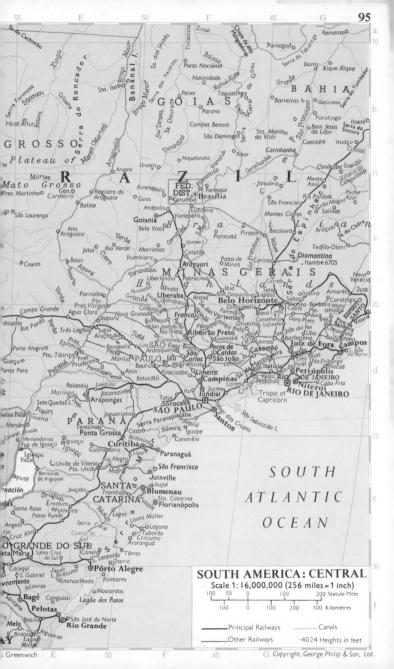

SOUTH AMERICA: CENTRAL

Scale 1:16,000,000 (256 miles = 1 inch)

100   50   0   100   200 Statute Miles

100   0   100   200   300 Kilometres

——— Principal Railways   ······· Canals

——— Other Railways   ·4024 Heights in feet

Copyright, George Philip & Son, Ltd.

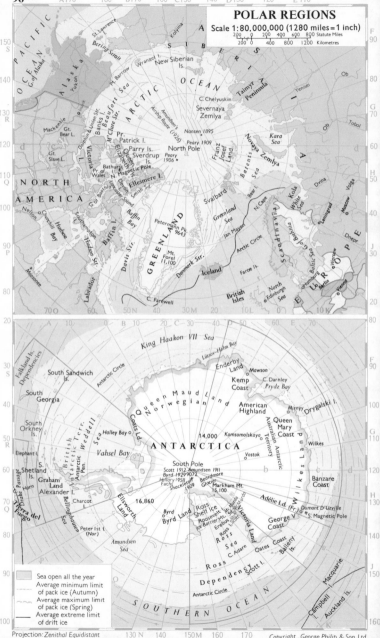

A170   180   B170   160   C150   140   D130   120   E110

POLAR REGIONS
Scale 1:80,000,000 (1280 miles = 1 inch)

200   0   200 400 600 800 Statute Miles
200   0   400   800   1200 Kilometres

PACIFIC OCEAN
G. of Alaska
St. Lawrence I.
Bering Strait
New Siberian Is.
Wrangel I.
Kolyma
SIBERIA
Alaska
Yukon
Pt. Barrow
Beaufort Sea
C. Chelyuskin
Taimyr Peninsula
Ob
Yenisei
Tobol
ARCTIC OCEAN
Mackenzie
Amundsen
McClure Str.
Banks I.
Amundsen Route (1928)
Nansen 1895
Severnaya Zemlya
Kara Sea
Gt. Bear L.
Dolphin & Union Str.
Pr. Patrick I.
Parry Is.
Sverdrup Is.
Peary 1909
North Pole
Peary 1906
Franz Josef Land
Novaya Zemlya
Gt. Slave L.
Victoria I.
Bathurst I.
Pr. of Wales I.
N. Magnetic Pole
Barents Sea
NORTH
Pr. of Wales I.
G. of Boothia
Ellesmere I.
Bear I.
N. Cape
Kola Pen.
White Sea
Dvina
AMERICA
Lancaster Sound
Smith Sd.
Devon I.
Svalbard
Jan Mayen
Kola
Leningrad
Moscow
Volga
Nelson
Churchill
Hudson Bay
Baffin Bay
Greenland Sea
Arctic Circle
EUROPE
Dnepr
Labrador
Southampton I.
Hudson Str.
Baffin I.
Davis Str.
GREENLAND
Petermann Pk. 9643
Mt. Forel 11,100
Denmark Str.
Faroe Is.
North Sea
Hamburg
Berlin
Warsaw
Vienna
Moose
C. Farewell
Iceland
British Isles
Edinburgh

70   60   50N   40   50M   60   40L   30   20K   10   0

80   F   90   140   150S   130   R   120   d   110   Q   100   P   90

70   80   G   90   60   H   50   J   40   30   20

20   10   0   80   30S   40   50R   60   70   80   90   100

A   10   20   B   C   30   40   D   50   60   E   70

King Haakon VII Sea
Lützow-Holm Bay
Enderby Land
Mawson
C. Darnley
Prydz Bay
American Highland
Mirnyy
Drygalski I.
Falkland Is. Dependencies
South Sandwich Is.
South Georgia
Antarctic Circle
Kemp Coast
Queen Maud Land
Norwegian
Norwegian Sea
Queen Mary Coast
South Orkney Is.
Coats Ld.
Halley Bay
14,000
Komsomolskaya
Australian Antarctic Territory
Wilkes
Elephant I.
British Antarctic Terr.
Antarctic Pen.
Weddell Sea
ANTARCTICA
Vostok
Wilkes Land
Banzare Coast
S. Shetland Is.
Vahsel Bay
South Pole
Scott 1912 Amundsen 1911
Byrd 1929 90 72
Jeffery 1958
Fuchs
Shackleton 1909
Beardmore Gl.
Markham Mt. 15,100
Graham Land
Alexander I.
Charcot
Drake Passage
Horn
Bellingshausen Sea
16,860
Byrd Land
Roosevelt I.
Ice Barrier Mt.
Beardmore Gl.
Adélie Ld. (Fr.)
Dumont D'Urville
S. Magnetic Pole
Tierra del Fuego
Ellsworth Land
Byrd
Ross Shelf Ice
Ross
Erebus
Ross Sea
Victoria Land
George V Coast
Oates Coast
Peter 1st I. (Nor.)
Amundsen Sea
C. Adare
C. Colbeck
Ross Dependency
Scott I.
Balleny Is.
Macquarie I.
SOUTHERN OCEAN
Antarctic Circle
Campbell I.
Auckland Is.

90   100   110   120   130   140   150   160

30S   F   90   40   100   50R   G   110   60   120   70   H   130   80   140   90   J   150   100   160

130 N   140   150M   160   170

Sea open all the year
Average minimum limit of pack ice (Autumn)
Average maximum limit of pack ice (Spring)
Average extreme limit of drift ice

Projection: Zenithal Equidistant

Copyright, George Philip & Son, Ltd.

INDEX

ABBREVIATIONS

Afr. – Africa
Ala. – Alabama
Arch. – Archipelago
Arg. – Argentina
Aust. – Austria
Austral. – Australia
Aut. Reg. – Autonomous Region
B. – Bay, Bight
Beds. – Bedfordshire
Belg. – Belgium
Bol. – Bolivia
Braz. – Brazil
C. – Cape
Calif. – California
Can. – Canada
Cant. – Canton
Chan. – Channel
Co. – County
Col. – Colombia, Colony
Conn. – Connecticut
C. Prov. – Cape Province
cont. – Continent
Cord. – Cordillera
Dépt. – Department
Des. – Desert
Dist. – District
div. – Division
Dom. Rep. – Dominican Republic
E. – East
Eg. – Egypt
Eng. – England
Fed. – Federation
Fd. – Fjord
Fla. – Florida
Fr. – France, French
G. – Gulf, Gebel

Ga. – Georgia
Gam. – Gambia
Ger. – Germany
Guin. – Guinea
Harb. – Harbour, Harbor
Hd. – Head
I.(s) – Island(s)
Ill. – Illinois
Ind. – Indiana
Ire. – Ireland
Jam. – Jamaica
Jap. – Japan
Jc., Junc. – Junction
Kan. – Kansas
King. – Kingdom
Ky. – Kentucky
L. – Lake, Lough, Loch
La. – Louisiana
Lab. – Labrador
Lancs. – Lancashire
Ld. – Land
Lib. – Liberia
Mad. P. – Madhya Pradesh
Mass. – Massachusetts
Md. – Maryland
Me. – Maine
Mex. – Mexico
Mich. – Michigan
Minn. – Minnesota
Miss. – Mississippi
Mo. – Missouri
Mor. – Morocco
Mozam. – Mozambique
Mt. – Mountain, Mount
Mts. – Mountains
Nat. – Natal
N.B. – New Brunswick
N.C. – North Carolina
Neb. – Nebraska

Neth. – Netherlands
Nev. – Nevada
Newf. – Newfoundland
N. Guin. – New Guinea
N.H. – New Hampshire
Nic. – Nicaragua
Nig. – Nigeria
N.J. – New Jersey
Nor. – Norway
N.S.W. – New South Wales
N.Y. – New York
N.Z. – New Zealand
Okla. – Oklahoma
Ont. – Ontario
Ore. – Oregon
P. – Paso, Pass
Pa. – Pennsylvania
Pak. – Pakistan
Par. – Paraguay
Pen. – Peninsula
Pk. – Peak
Plat. – Plateau
Pol. – Poland
Port. – Portugal
Pref. – Prefecture
Prot. – Protectorate
Prov. – Province
Pta. – Punta
Queens. – Queensland
R. – River
Ra. – Range
Raj. – Rajasthan
Reg. – Region
Rep. – Republic
Res. – Reservoir
Rhod. – Rhodesia
S. – Sea, South
Sa. – Sierra, Serra

S.C. – South Carolina
Scot. – Scotland
S.D. – South Dakota
Sd. – Sound
Sen. – Senegal
Somal. – Somaliland, Somali Republic
Sp., Span. – Spain, Spanish
S.S.R. – Soviet Socialist Republic
st. – state
Str. – Strait
Swed. – Sweden
Switz. – Switzerland
Tas. – Tasmania
Tenn. – Tennessee
Terr. – Territory
Tex. – Texas
Trans. – Transvaal
Tur. – Turkey
Ut. P. – Uttar Pradesh
U.S.A. – United States of America
U.S.S.R. – Union of Soviet Socialist Republics
Va. – Virginia
Ven. – Venezuela
Vic. – Victoria
Vol. – Volcano
Vt. – Vermont
W. – West, Wadi
Wash. – Washington
W. Austral. – Western Australia
W. Ind. – West Indies
Wis. – Wisconsin
W. Va. – West Virginia
Wyo. – Wyoming
Yorks. – Yorkshire

3

* Renamed N' gage   * Renamed Kirimati

* Renamed Kaga Bandoro   * Renamed Dhaka & Div.   * Renamed Antsiranana

* Renamed Faradofay
† Renamed Masvingo
‡ Renamed Xangongo
* Renamed Iqaluit
* Renamed Kadoma
* Renamed Kiribati

* Renamed Gweru   * Renamed Chegutu

* Renamed L. Edward

43 Jask Hd
30 Jaszbereny Cb
95 Jau Fd
47 Jaunpur Jf
48 Java, I. & Sea Bd
42 Jaynagar Le
73 Jazin Bc
8 Jedburgh Fe
22 Jedrzejow Fc
86 Jefferson City Bd
73 Jegega Gb
51 Jelenia Góra Cc
32 Jelgava Dd
17 Jena Dc
91 Jeremie Dc
26 Jerez Ab
62 Jericho, Austral. Cc
62 Jericho, Jordan Bd
14 Jersey, I. Bc
89 Jersey City Hd
48 Jerusalem Bd
28 Jerzu Bc
49 Jesselton, see Kota Kinabalu
47 Jessore Mg
47 Jeypore Jj
46 Jhang Maghiana Cc
46 Jhansi Ec
46 Jhelum Db
46 Jhunjhunu Ed
42 Jidda Cd
22 Jihlava Cd
73 Jima Fd
30 Jimbolia Cc
90 Jimenez Db
73 Jinja Ec
40 Jinotega Ad
40 Jisr ash Shughur Cb

51 Joanna Spring Cc
92 João Pessoa Fe
22 Joblonec Cc
46 Jodhpur De
92 Joeuf Fe
62 Jogjakarta Cd
75 Johannesburg Dc
8 John-o-Groats Eb
88 Johnson City, Tenn. Df
89 Johnson City, N.Y. Gc
8 Johnstone De
89 Johnstown, Pa. Fd
89 Johnstown, N.Y. Hc
48 Johore Bahru Bc
20 Joigny Bb
95 Joinville Fe
10 Jokkmokk Db
8 Jolie Bd
81 Joliette Bb
79 Jones Sd. Ja
30 Jonesboro Bd
81 Jonkoping Cd
81 Jonquière Bb
91 Joplin Bd
21 Jordan, king. Hf
40 Jordan, R. Bc
10 Jörn Eb
41 Jos Gg
8 Juan de Fuca, Str. Bc
57 Juan Fernandez Is.
73 Juba Ba
26 Juba, R. Gc
70 Juby, C. Cc
20 Júcar, R. Bb
91 Jucaro Cc
10 Juist Fa
95 Juiz de Fora Fe
94 Jujuy Bd
73 Julfa Jh
94 Juli Bc
94 Juliaca Ad
78 Julianehaab Nb
41 Jullundur Ec
19 Jumet Dd
41 Jumla Jd
43 Junagadh Ch
94 Junction City Cd
95 Jundiai Fd
82 Juneau Ec
61 Junee Cb
43 Jungfrau, mt. Cb
44 Juniyah Bc
73 Jur, R. Db
8 Jura, I. Ce
20 Jura, mts. & dept. Dc
94 Juruena Db
43 Jylland Cc

44 K2 (Mt. Godwin Austen Da
74 Kaap Plat Cc
71 Kabala Cd
71 Kabale Ed
74 Kabalo De
73 Kabarega Falls De
72 Kabongo De
72 Kabompo, R. Cf
44 Kabul Gg

45 Kachin, st. Hc
71 Kaddi Cd
60 Kadina Ab
73 Kadugli Da
41 Kaduna Gf
71 Kaedi Ce
74 Kafanchan Bd
55 Kafia Kingi Cb
22 Kafue, R. Dd
55 Kagawa, pref. Bd
55 Kagoshima, B. Bd
55 Kagoshima, I. Cc
83b Kahoolawe, I. Cb
67 Kaiapoi De
51 Kaifeng Fc
66 Kaikohe Da
67 Kaikoura De
66 Kaimanawa Mts. Fc
70 Kairouan Ga
51 Kaiserslautern Ge
66 Kaitaia Da
66 Kaitangata Bg
10 Kajaani Fc
71 Kajan R. Cc
73 Kakamega Ec
74 Kakamos Cc
10 Kakau Veld Cb
55 Kalabagh Cb
37 Kalabaka Bb
53 Kalach He
74 Kalahari, des. Cb
55 Kalámata Bb
55 Kalamazoo Cc
44 Kalat Bc
46 Kalat-i-Ghilzai Bb
73 Kalemie (Albertville) Cb
51 Kaigan Fb
65 Kalgoorlie Ce *
51 Kalima Bd
48 Kalimantan Cd
37 Kalimnos, I. Cb
32 Kalinin Gd
38 Kaliningrad (Konigsberg) De
22 Kalisz Ec
73 Kaliua Ec
73 Kalmar Dc
30 Kalocsa Bb
75 Kalomo Da
29 Kaluga Ge
55 Kama Ec
35 Kamaishi Dc
39 Kamaran Is. Dd
73 Kambi De
55 Kamchatka Pen. Td
32 Kamenets Podolskiy Ef
33 Kamensk-Shakhtinski Hf
72 Kamina De
35 Kamloops Bb
48 Kampar R. Bc
48 Kampen Eb
48 Kampot Bb
48 Kamsack Db
55 Kamuitaki, Mt. Db
73 Kamyshin Je
72 Kanagawa, pref. Cc
72 Kananga (Luluabourg) Ce
44 Kanash Jd
44 Kanazawa Cc
44 Kancheepuram Df
47 Kanchenjunga, mt. Le
51 Kanchow Fc
44 Kanda Kanda Cd
46 Kandaghat Fc
44 Kandahar Bb
32 Kandalaksha & L. Fb
48 Kandangan Cd
66 Kandavu, I. Gk
73 Kandersteg Bb
71 Kandi Ff
44 Kandla Cg
47 Kandy Dg
62 Kangaroo I. Ec
31 Kangean Is. Cd
88 Kankakee Bd
21 Kankan Df
34 Kanin, C. Hb
71 Kano Gf
65 Kanowna Ce
43 Kansas, st. Bd
90 Kanpur He
51 Kansas, st. Dc
86 Kansas City Bd
51 Kansk Md
50-51 Kansu, prov. Ec
31 Kántó, dist. Ec
55 Kanturk Cc
51 Kaohsiung Gd
74 Kaoko-Otavi Aa
74 Kaoko Veld Aa
52 Kapanga Ce

28 Kapela, mts. Eb
73 Kapoeta Ec
24 Kaposvar Ab
48 Kapuas R. Bd
46 Kapunda Ab
34 Kara Kum Des. He
3 Kara Sea Ja
55 Karachev Ge
44 Karachi Bd
34 Karaganda Ke
55 Karaikal Df
49 Karakelog Bc
55 Karakoram Ra. & P.,
74 Karamai Cb
50 Karaman Db
67 Karamea B. Cd
74 Karasburg Bc
10 Karasjok Fb
55 Karasu Da
55 Karatsu Cc
28 Katawanken, mts. Ea
42 Karbala Ec
30 Karcag Cb
77 Kardhitsa Bb
74 Kareeberge, mts. Cd
10 Karesuando Eb
73 Kariba Gorge & Lake Da
74 Karibib Ab
48 Karimata Is. Bd
48 Karimata str. Bd
22 Karimnagar Gj
42 Karkar I. Gg
41 Karkheh, R. Fc
17 Karl-Marx-Stadt Ec
28 Karlovac Ec
55 Karlovy Vary Bc
11 Karlskrona Dd
51 Karlsruhe He
11 Karlstad Cd
44 Karnal Fd
31 Karnobat st. Fd
73 Karonga Ee
73 Karora Cd
27 Karpathós, I. Cb
44 Karsakpai Je
64 Kartuzy Ea
73 Karungu Ed
22 Karvina Bd
41 Karwar Cf
25 Kas Cb
51 Kasai, R. Bd
55 Kasama Ef
73 Kasanga Ee
73 Kasangulu Bd
73 Kasenga Df
43 Kashan Ec
60 Kashgar Ad
54 Kashiwazaki Cc
46 Kashmor Bd
33 Kasimov He
11 Kaskinen Ec
72 Kasongo Lunda Be
27 Kasos, I. Cb
33 Kassala Cd
10 Kassel Cc
27 Kastamonu Da
33 Kastoronoye Ge
27 Kastellorizon, I., see Megiste Cb
46 Kasur Ec
72 Katako Kombe Cd
73 Katanning Be
33 Katerini Ba
32 Katherine La
44 Katihar Lf
47 Katima Rapids Ca
73 Katiola Dg
46 Katmandu Ke
72 Katompe De
72 Katoomba Db
22 Katowice Ec
27 Katsina Gf
33 Kattegat Ec
18 Katwijk-aan-Zee Db
57 Kauai I. Ab
21 Kaufbeuren Jh
76 Kaukdura Ab
46 Kaulirunta Eb
10 Kaunas Dd
73 Kavala Bd
43 Kawagoe Cc
73 Kawaguchi Cc
73 Kawambwa De
55 Kawasaki Cc
55 Kawerau Fc
66 Kawhia Harb. Ec
45 Kawthoolei, st. He
71 Kayes Cf
37 Kayseri Eb
44 Kazakhstan He
32 Kazan Jd
31 Kazanluk Ed

43 Kazerun Gd
72 Kazumba Ce
75 Kazungula Da
27 Kéa Bb
70 Kecskemet Bb
48 Kediri Cd
73 Kédougou Cf
3 Keeling Is., see Cocos Is. Mf
51 Keelung Gd
89 Keene Jc
62 Keerweer C. Ba
74 Keetmanshoop Bc
55 Kefallinia Bb
50 Kefar Ata Bc
10 Keflavik Ab
79 Keith, Austral. Bc
8 Keith, Scotland Fc
55 Keksgolm Fc
48 Kelantan R. Bc
72 Kellé Ad
72 Kelibberrin Be
72 Kellogg Cb
10 Kelloselka Hb
9 Kelis, see Caenannus Mor
55 Kelowna Cc
67 Kelso Bf
32 Kem Cd
34 Kemerovo Ld
10 Kemijärvi Fb
21 Kempen Ib
61 Kempsey Db
21 Kempten Jb
27 Kendrapara Lh
72 Kenhardt Cc
73 Kenitra Db
9 Kenmare & R. Be
24 Kennewick Cb
60 Kenora Ec
44 Kenosha Ec
32 Kent, co. Hf
48 Kentland Bd
83 Kentucky, st. Ec
78 Kentville Cb
66 Kenya, st. Ff
32 Kenya, Mt. Fd
73 Kenya, mt. Fd
86 Keokuk Bc
72 Keppel B. Dc
44 Kerala, st. Df
73 Kerang Bc
62 Kerch Gf
73 Kerchoual Fe
72 Kerema Gh
72 Kerets, C. Gb
21 Kerguelen, I. Lh
72 Kerintji, mt. Bd
55 Kerkenna Is. Ed
70 Kerkenna Is. Hb
27 Kérkira (Corfu) Ab
18 Kerkrade Fd
55 Kermadec Is. Ee
43 Kerman Hc
† 43 Kermanshah Fc
80 Kerrobert Db
9 Kerry, co. Bd
72 Kerulen Dd
55 Kesennuma Dc
8 Kessock Dc
72 Kestenga Fb
27 Keta Fg
33 Ketapang Bd
82a Ketchikan Ec
71 Kete Krachi Eg
21 Kettering Ge
55 Kewanee Cc
88 Kewaunee Bb
55 Keweenaw B. Cb
54 Key West Bb
66 Khabarov Mb
72 Khabarovo Jc
73 Khabarovsk Qe
72 Khaibar Db
72 Khairagarh Hh
46 Khairpur Bb
77 Khalkidhiki, pref. Ba
27 Khalkis Bb
72 Khaluin Jd
39 Khamis Mushait Dd
34 Khan Tengri, mt. Le
81 Khanagar Hh
46 Khandwa Fh
43 Khanewal Ec
50 Khangai, mts. Db
44 Khania Bb
46 Khanpur Cd
46 Kharagpur Lg
43 Kharg I. Gd
55 Kharga Oasis Cc
47 Kharovsk Hc
39 Kharoun Cd
55 Khashm el Girba Cd
31 Khaskovo Ee
35 Khatanga Nb

46 Khavda Bg
46 Khed Brahma Df
70 Khemis Miliana (Affreville) Fa
70 Khenchela Ga
33 Kherson Ff
55 Khetrisinring Dc
55 Khiok Od
27 Khios Cb
34 Khiva Je
35 Khmelnskiy Ef
32 Kholm Fd
55 Khoim, see Chelm Fd
51 Khongsomba Gb
33 Khoper R. He
43 Khorramshahr Fc
50 Khotan Bc
70 Khouritiga Db
74 Khuis Cb
47 Khulna Mg
43 Khurasan, reg. Hc
46 Khushab Db
44 Khyber P. Cb
51 Kiama Db
51 Kiamusze Hb
51 Kian Fd
51 Kiangsi, prov. Fd
51 Kiangsu Fc
72 Kibangou Ad
72 Kibombo Dd
80 Kicking Horse P., Cb
52 Kichmengski-Gorodok Jd
71 Kidal Fe
7 Kidderminster Ge
16 Kiel, & B. Da
22 Kielce Fc
51 Kienow Fd
51 Kienshui Ed
55 Kieta Ih
33 Kiev Fe
62 Kikori Fh
52 Kilchu Ba
9 Kildare, & co. Ec
73 Kilembe Ec
55 Kilikee Bd
73 Kilkeel Eb
9 Kilkenny & co, Dd
73 Kilialoe Bc
9 Killarney Bd
9 Killiney Ec
9 Killybegs Cb
9 Kilmatlock Cd
8 Kilmarnock Ee
8 Kilmuir Bc
8 Kilrush Bd
73 Kilwa Kisiwani Fe
73 Kilwa Kivinje Fe
65 Kimba Fe
75 Kimberley Dc
54 Kimberley, dist. Db
32 Kimry Gd
82 Kinabalu, mt. Cc
73 Kindia Cg
74 Kindu Dd
33 Kineshma Hd
64 King Bay, see Dampier
51 King I. Bd
34 King Sd. Cb
78 King Christian IX Land Oa
78 King Frederik VI Land Na
66 King George Sd. Bf
78 King William I, Hb
75 King William's Town Dd
63 Kingaroy Dd
9 King's Lynn He
73 Kingsbridge Dg
63 Kingston, Australia Ac
46 Kingston, Can. Bb
91 Kingston, Jam. Cc
89 Kingston, N.Z. Bf
Kingston, U.S.A.
33 Kingstown Fd
81 Kingsville Cd
51 Kingtehchen Fd
79 Kinya Kb
72 Kinkala Ad
55 Kinki, dist. Cd
66 Kinleith Fc
8 Kinloch Rannoch Dd
8 Kinnaird's Hd. Fc
8 Kinross Ed
9 Kinsale Ce
72 Kinshasa Be

* Renamed Kalgoorlie-Boulder   † Renamed Bakhtaran

*Renamed Chemnitz

8 Kintore Fc
3 Kintyre, dist. Ce
27 Kiparissia Bb
72 Kipushi Dd
51 Kir, prov. Gb
35 Kirensk Nd
34 Kirgizia Kf
71 Kirin Gb
62 Kiriwini Is. Hh
8 Kirkcaldy Ed
46 Kirklee Dj
10 Kirkenes Fb
71 Kirklareli Ca
8 Kirkmichael Ed
42 Kirkuk Eb
8 Kirkwall Fb
32 Kirov Jd
33 Kirovabad Jg
33 Kirovograd Hf
32 Kirovsk Fb
Kirriemuir Ed
33 Kirsanov He
71 Kirşehir Db
10 Kiruna Eb
72 Kirundu Bd
72 Kiryu Cc
55 Kisangani Dc
55 Kisarazu Cd
46 Kishangarh Ce
33 Kishinev Ef
54 Kishiwada Cd
46 Kishtwar Eb
55 Kisi Hb
73 Kisiju Fe
30 Kiskőrös Bb
30 Kiskunfelegy-haza Bb
30 Kiskunhalas Bb
73 Kismayu Gd
25 Kiso, R. Cc
30 Kisujszállas Cb
54 Kitakami, R. Dc
55 Kitakyūshū Bd

73 Kitale Fc
54 Kitami Db
81 Kitchener Ed
47 Kithira, I. Bb
27 Kithnos, I. Bb
70 Kitimat Bb
53 Kitwe Df
17 Kitzingen Dd
51 Kiukiang Fd
23 Kivu, L. Dd
32 Kizel Ld
32 Kizil, R. Da
33 Kiziyar Jg
32 Kladno Cc
33 Klagenfurt He
32 Klaipeda Bd
84 Klamath Falls Bc
51 Klaohsien Fc
74 Klausen P. Cb
74 Klawer Bd
75 Klerksdorp Dc
33 Kietskaya Hf
8 Kleve Fc
32 Klin Gd
52 Klobuck Ec
32 Klodzko Dc
78 Klondike Db
17 Klosterneuburg Gd
13 Klosters Db
55 Klyuchevsk Vol.Td
7 Knighton Ed
17 Knittelfeld Fe
31 Knokke Cc
88 Knoxville Df
74 Knysna Cd
28 Kobaric Da
55 Kobayashi Bd
55 Kobe Cd
62 KöbenhavnsCo.Fd
19 Koblenz Bd
25 Kocevje Eb
55 Kochi & pref. Bd
82a Kodiak & I. Cc
71 Koforidua Eg
75 Kofu Cc
52 Köge Fd
54 Kogota Dc
44 Kohat Cb
45 Kohima Gc
55 Kojima Bd
55 Kojonup Be
34 Kokand Ke
34 Kokchetav Jd
65 Kokiu Ed
10 Kokkola Ec
55 Kokomo Bd
55 Kokura Bd
52 Kola Ec
44 Kola Pen. Gb
44 Kolar Df
46 Kolayat (Srikolayabji) De
71 Kolda Cd
12 Kolding Cd
49 Kolepom I. Fg
52 Kolguyev Jb
34 Kolguyev I. Gc
47 Kolhapur Cd
22 Kolin Cd

18 Köln, see Cologne Gd
22 Kolo Eb
22 Kolozeeg Ca
31 Kolokani Df
32 Kolomna Cd
72 Kolwezi Df
25 Kolyma R. & Ra. Sc
35 Komandorskiye Is. Td
22 Komárno Ee
75 Komatipoort Ec
55 Komatsushima Bd
27 Komotini Ca
48 Kompong Cham Bb
48 Kompong Som Bb
55 Komsomolets I. Ma
33 Komsomolsk I. Ma
96 Komsomolska-ya Fb
35 Komsomolsk Ud
32 Kondopoga Fc
10 Konginge Bb
53 Kongmoon Fd
72 Kongolo De
13 Kongsberg Bd
22 Konin Ec
25 Konjic Fc
72 Konosha Hc
72 Konotop Fe
22 Konskie Fc
32 Konstantin-ovski Hf
13 Kontanz Da
27 Kontar Hb
30 Konya Db
73 Konza Fd
22 Koper Db
12 Kopervik Bd
33 Koprinvica Fa
55 Korat, see Nakhon Ratchasima
18 Korback Hc
17 Korce Ba
81 Korcula, I. Fc
37 Korea, N. & S. Reps. Cc
85 Korea Str. Bb
27 Korinthos Bb
55 Korityrna De
77 Korkuteli Db
22 Kornat, I. Fc
66 Koro S. Hk
32 Koroit Bc
33 Korsakov Re
60 Korsør Ed
13 Korsun Ff
18 Kortrijk Cd
60 Kosamburra C9
27 Kos, I. Cb
12 Koscian Db
62 Kosciusko, mt. Cc
33 Košice Fd
55 Kosti Cd
52 Kostroma Hd
52 Kostrzyn Cb
33 Kosvenski Kamen Da
22 Kostalin Da
30 Koszeg Ab
46 Kota Ef
48 Kota Bharu Bc
49 Kota Kinabalu Cd
72 Kote Cd
32 Kotelnich Jd
55 Koteinikovski Hf
11 Kotka Fc
52 Kotlas Jc
46 Kotri Db
46 Kotor Bd
75 Kotuy R. Nb
32 Kouango Cb
70 Koudougou Ef
71 Kouroussa Df
33 Kovel Ee
32 Kovik Kb
72 Kovrhd Gc
55 Kowloon Fd
47 Kozáni Df
54 Kozhikode Df
32 Koztva Lb
22 Kozianice Fc
52 Kozmin Dc
71 Kpandu Fg
11 Kragero Bd
32 Kragujevac Cc
48 Kraikania I. Bd
51 Krakow (Cracow) Ec
33 Králicky Sneznik, mt. Dc
30 Kraljevo Cd
33 Kramatorsk Gf
74 Kranskop Ec
52 Krasnik Fc
33 Krasnoarmeisk Je
52 Krasnodar Cd
52 Krasnokamsk Ld

32 Krasnoufimsk Ld
34 Krasnovodsk Hd
45 Krasnoyarsk Md
33 Krasny He
34 Krasny Kut Je
22 Krasnytaw Gc
46 Kratie Bb
15 Krefeld Fb
33 Kremenchug Ff
17 Krems Fd
69 Kribi De
44 Krishna R. De
44 Krishnanagar Mg
11 Kristiansand Bd
10 Kristiansund Bc
11 Kristinehamn Cd
77 Kriti, see Crete Bb
51 Krivoy Rog Ff
87 Krk, I. Eb
22 Krkonose (Giant) Mts. Cc
22 Kromeriz Dd
10 Kromfors Db
22 Kronshtadt Fd
11 Kronstaad Dc
33 Kropotkin Hf
72 Krosno Fd
22 Krotoszyn Dc
55 Krško Eb
75 Krugersdorp Dc
22 Krumlov Cd
50 Krusevac Cd
22 Krzepioz Ec
30 Ksar el Kebir Db
48 Kuala Lipis Bc
48 Kuala Lumpur Bc
48 Kuala Selangor Bc
48 Kuala Trengganu Bc
35 Kuba Jg
22 Kuban Gd
50 Kucha Cb
48 Kuching Cc
46 Kuda Df
46 Kudus Cd
72 Kudymkar Kc
73 Kuh-e-Hazaran, mt. Hd
10 Kuhmo Fc
10 Kuivaniemi Fb
54 Kuji Db
70 Kuldja Cb
60 Kulwin Bb
71 Kuma Hf
46 Kuma R. Jg
54 Kumamoto & pref. Bd
44 Kumara Ce
71 Kumasi Eg
44 Kumbakonam Df
46 Kunch Gf
55 Kungho Bc
32 Kungur Ld
50 Kunlun Shan, mts. Cc
55 Kunming Ed
52 Kunsan Bb
52 Kuopio Fc
33 Kupang De
33 Kupyansk Gf
44 Kura R. Jg
75 Kurashiki Bd
47 Kurdistan, reg. Db
55 Kure Bd
74 Kurgan Jd
72 Kuria Muria, Is. Ed
10 Kuril Is. Se
32 Kurland Bd
46 Kurnool De
67 Kurow Cf
46 Kurrikurri Db
55 Kursk Ge
71 Kursmilija Cd
44 Kuruman & R. Cc
55 Kurume Bd
32 Kurya Ef
72 Kushiro Db
58 Kushka Ff
44 Kushtia Mg
13 Kussnacht Ca
27 Kütahya Cb
33 Kutaisi Hg
46 Kutch, Gulf of Bg
72 Kutu Bd
68 Kutum Ad
33 Kuvandyk Le
45 Kuwait, st. Fd
34 Kuwana Cc
33 Kuybyshev Ke
79 Kuznetsk Je
32 Kuzomen Gb
55 Kwangchow Fd
55 Kwangju Bb
51 Kwangsi-Chuang Aut. Dist. Ed
55 Kwangtung Ed
52 Kwangtung, prov. Fc
51 Kweichow, prov. Ed
51 Kwetiin Fd
51 Kweiyang Ed
22 Kwidzyn Db

72 Kyabe Bb
35 Kyakhta Nd
45 Kyaukse Hd
8 Kyle of Lochalsh Cc
60 Kyneton Bc
54 Kyo, C. Cc
73 Kyoga, L. Ec
61 Kyogle Da
52 Kyongju Bb
54 Kyoto & pref. Cc
54 Kyttym Ld
55 Kyushu, I. & dist. Bd
31 Kyustendil Dd
34 Kyzyl Kum Des. Je
34 Kzyl Orda Je

21 La Bochetta P. Ge
91 La Ceiba Ac
13 La Chaux de Fonds Aa
92 La Chorrera Dc
74 La Coruña Aa
86 La Crosse Bc
88 La Esperanza Cb
26 La Estrada Aa
88 La Fayette Bd
88 La Folette Cf
70 La Goulette Ha
6 La Grange Cb
20 La Grand Combe Ce
92 La Guaira Ca
75 La Linea Ab
19 La Louvière Dd
16 La Mancha, dist. Bb
93 La Pampa, prov. Cf
92 La Paragua Cb
92 La Paz, Bolivia Dc
14 La Paz, Par. Df
90 La Paz, R. Bb
93 La Plata, R. de la Df
71 Labe Cc
22 Labe (Elbe) R. Db
75 Labrador Lc
48 Labuan, I. Cc
73 Labuha Dd
47 Labuk B. Cc
80 Lac la Biche Cb
32 Lac Jeannine Ca
70 Lacaune, Mts. de Af
44 Laccadive Is. Cf
13 Lachen Ca
81 Lachine Bb
60 Lachlan R. Bb
89 Laconia Kc
22 Ladis Jd
74 Ladismith Cd
32 Ladoga, L. Fc
40 Ladrone Is, see Mariana Is.
75 Ladybrand Dc
80 Ladysmith, Canada Cc
74 Ladysmith, Natal Dc
11 Lahti Fc
68 Lai Ad
72 Laidley Da
43 Laila He
74 Laingsburg Cd
87 Lake Charles Be
17 Lake City De
85 Lake Ghazie Dc
79 Lake Harbour Lb
87 Lakeland Df
68 Lakes Entrance Cc
88 Lakewood Ed
46 Lakhimpur He
46 Lakhpat Bg
10 Lakselv Ea
51 Lakshadweep Is. Cf
17 Lalitpur Gf
9 Lambay I. Ec
28 Lame De
26 Lamego, R. Aa
27 Lámia Bb
64 Limmen Bight Fa

7 Lampeter Ce
73 Lamu Gd
83b Lanai, I. Cb
6 Lanark Ce
6 Lancashire, co. Ed
6 Lancaster Ec
79 Lancaster Sd. Ia
75 Lanchow Ec
13 Landana Ae
7 Landeck De
15 Landes, dept. De
21 Landsberg Ja
7 Land's End Bg
17 Landshut Ed
10 Landskrona Ca
74 Langeberge, mt.Cc
12 Langeland De
13 Langenthal Ba
18 Langeoog, I. Ga
8 Langholm Ed
75 Langkloof Mts. Cd
10 Langoy, I. Db
13 Langres Cb
13 Langres, Plat. Cb
10 Langsele Dc
20 Languedoc, dist. Hf
55 Lansing Cc
58 Lanusei Bc
70 Lanzarote, I. Cc
40 Laoag Db
9 Laoighis, co. Dd
14 Laon Ec
45 Laos, st. Bb
88 Lapper Dc
10 Lapland, region Fb
43 Lapua Ec
23 Lapy Gb
43 Lar Gd
74 Larache Da
84 Laramie Ec
85 Laredo Gf
28 Larino Ed
27 Larisa Bb
86 Larkana Be
5 Larne Fb
11 Larvik Bd
20 Larzac, Causse du, mts. Bf
85 Las Cruces Ef
39 Las Khoreh Dd
85 Las Palmas Ac
58 Las Plumas Cg
90 Las Tres Marias, Is. Cc
85 Las Vegas, New Mexico Fd
45 Lashio Hd
7 Lask Ec
40 Latakia (Al Ladhiqiyah) Db
29 Latina Dd
8 Latheron Eb
61 Latrobe Ed
22 Latvia Bd
66 Lau or Eastern Group, Is. Hk
8 Laude z Fe
13 Laufen Ba
Launceston, England
61 Launceston,Tas.Cd
62 Laura Bb
87 Laurel Ce
88 Laurium Cb
13 Lauro Müller Fe
13 Lausanne Ab
47 Laut I. Cd
14 Laval Cc
55 Laverton Cd
11 Lavik Bc
95 Lawra Cd
71 Lawers Cd
71 Lawra Af
15 Lawrence, Kan. Ad
89 Lawrence,Mass.Kc
67 Lawrence, N.Z. Bf
85 Lawton Gc
11 Laxa Cd
56 Laysan I. Kb
29 Lazio, prov. Dd
20 le Chambon-Feugerolles Cd
15 Le Creusot Fd
14 Le Havre Cc
70 Le Kef Ga
13 Le Locle Aa
15 Le Mans Cc
12 Le Marinel Df
20 Le Puy Bd
14 Le Tréport Db
84 Leadville Ed
8 Lealui Eg
88 Leamington, Canada Dc
7 Leamington, England Fe
6 Learmonth Ac
86 Leavenworth Ad

* Renamed Cacongo

* Renamed Shah Faisalabad
† Renamed Talien (Lüta)
* Renamed Bioko
† Renamed Mafikeng
‡ Renamed Mahajanga

* Renamed Vanuatu

* Renamed Mucunda
† Renamed Ngunza

* Renamed Belau

60 Rope Ac
74 Robertson Dd
71 Robertsport Cg
60 Robertstown Ab
81 Roberval Bb
26 Roca, C. da Ab
93 Rocha Ed
6 Rochdale Ed
26 Rochefort Ce
86 Rochester, Minn. Bc
89 Rochester, N.Y. Gc
86 Rock Island Dd
84 Rock Springs Ec
89 Rocky Ford Fd
93 Rocky Mount Gg
84 Rocky Mts. Db
86 Rockford Cc
26 Rockhampton Dc
62 Rockingham B. Cb
11 Rodberg Bc
12 Rodbyhavn Ac
12 Rodez Ee
27 Ródhos (Rhodes), I. Cb
30 Rodna Eb
64 Roebourne Ab
64 Roebuck B. Cb
18 Roermond Ge
18 Roeselare Cd
70 Rogers City Db
74 Roggeveldberge, mts. Cd
10 Rognan Ed
46 Rohri Be
46 Rohtak Fd
70 Rojo, C. Ef
55 Rokugo, C. Cc
95 Rolandia Ed
63 Roma Fg
11 Romagna, reg. Cb
30 Roman Fb
21 Romanche, R. Ed
5 Romania, st. Kf
21 Rome, Italy Dd
89 Rome, U.S.A. Hc
7 Romford Hf
12 Romo, I. Bd
21 Ronda Ab
92 Rondônia, st. Cd
21 Rome Fa
12 Ronse Cd
89 Roosendaal Dc
96 Roosevelt I. La
92 Roraima, st. Cb
11 Röros Cc
23 Rorschach Da
10 Ros Vatn Cb
93 Rosario, Arg. Cf
91 Rosario, Mexico co. Cc
9 Roscrea Dc
18 Roseau Fc
39 Roseires Cd
18 Rosendael Bc
86 Roseneim Ee
81 Rosetown Db
6 Roskilde Fd
33 Rostavi Fe
7 Ross, England Ef
67 Ross, N.Z. Ce
96 Ross Dependency Lc
91 Ross I. Lb
96 Ross Sea Lb
96 Ross Shelf Ice La
80 Rossland Cf
9 Rosslare Ed
71 Rosso Ge
33 Rossosh Ge
31 Rostock Fa
33 Rostov Gf
95 Roswell Fc
8 Rosyth Ed
32 Rotenburg Ja
7 Rother Hg
6 Rotherham Fd
8 Rothsay Fe
60 Roto Cb
66 Rotorua Fc
18 Rotterdam Dc
21 Rottweil Ga
15 Kottuneroog, I. Fa
7 Rouen Dd
8 Rousay, I. Fa
15 Roussillon Ef
11 Rouyn Hd
21 Rovato Jd
21 Rovereto Kd
28 Rovigo Dc
28 Rovinj Db
33 Rovno Be
67 Roxburgh, N.Z. Bf
8 Roxburgh, co., Scotland Fe
47 Royagada Jj
8 Royale, I. Bb
7 Royston Ge
23 Roznava Fd
33 Rtishchevo He
65 Ruapehu, Mt. Ec

39 Rub al Khali, des. Dd
32 Rudnichny Kd
50 Rudok Bc
17 Rudolstadt Dc
48 Rudyard Ca
73 Rufiji, R. Fe
7 Rufisque Bf
7 Rugby Fe
16 Rügen, I. Ea
18 Ruhr, R. Fc
72 Ruki, R. Bd
73 Rukwa, L. Ee
30 Ruma Bc
73 Rumbek Db
54 Rumoi Db
50 Runanga Ce
75 Rusape Ec
19 Rush Ec
60 Rushworth Bc
30 Ruse Fd
27 Russellville Bd
† 34-35 Russian Soviet Federal Socialist Republic Lc
75 Rustenburg Dc
7 Rutland, co., England Ge
89 Rutland, U.S.A. Jc
73 Ruvuma, R. Ff
73 Ruwenzori, mt. Dc
73 Ruzaevka Je
23 Ruzomberok Ed
73 Rwanda, st. Dd
35 Ryazan Ge
33 Ryazhsk He
*32 Rybinsk Gd
32 Rybinsk Res. Gd
7 Ryde Fg
7 Rye Hg
32 Rynda Gb
23 Rzeszów Fc
23 Rzhev Fe

20 St. Claude Dc
86 St. Cloud Bc
91 St. Croix, I. Fc
23 St. Dié Gd
14 St. Dizier Df
20 St. Eloy Ac
20 St. Etienne Ce
20 St. Florentin Ba
13 St. Gallen Da
61 St. George, Australia Ce
85 St. George, U.S.A. Dd
91 St. George's Fg
9 St. George's Chan. Ee
19 St. Germain Bf
20 St. Germain des Fosses Bc
13 St. Gotthard P. Cb
12 St. Heddinge Fd
74 St. Helena, I. Bb
67 St. Helena, I. Bg
6 St. Helens Ed
81 St. Hyacinthe Bb
88 St. Ignace Cb
19 St. Ingbert Ge
7 St. Ives Bg
8 St. Jean Jb
89 St. Jerome Jb
21 Saint John Cb
91 St. John's, Antigua Fe
81 St. John's, Can. Db
88 St. Joseph, Mich. Bc
88 St. Joseph, Miss. Bd
15 St. Juan Gf
13 St. Julien Ab
67 St. Kilda Cf
91 St. Kitts, see St. Christopher Fc
62 St. Lawrence Cc
81 St. Lawrence, R. Cb
82a St. Lawrence I. Bb
81 St. Lawrence, R. Cb
14 St. Lô Cc
71 St. Louis, Sen. Be
91 St. Louis, U.S.A. Bd
91 St. Lucia, I. Fd
14 St. Maio Dc
91 St. Marc Dc
81 St. Martin, I. Fc
89 St. Marys Fd
60 St. Mary's Pk. Ab
14 St. Nazaire Bd
7 St. Neots Ge
8 St. Nicolas Eb
14 St. Omer Eb
20 St. Paul, French Guiana Db
86 St. Paul, U.S.A. Bc
2 St. Paul, I. Fd
87 St. Petersburg Df
31 St. Pierre I. De
18 St. Pol-sur-Mer Bc
27 St. Pölten Fd
14 St. Quentin Ee
15 St. Raphael Gf
84 St. Sebastian B. Cd
90 St. Felipe Bf
91 St. Thomas, I. Ec
38 St. Trond Ed
15 St. Tropez Gf
17 St. Veit Fe
84 St. Vincent, C. Ab
91 St. Vincent G. Ab
*91 St. Vincent, I. Fd
69 Ste. Marie, C. Dh
55 Saitama, pref. Cc
33 Sakai Cd
33 Sakaiminato Bc
42 Sakaka Ec
73 Sakania Df
55 Sakarya, R. Ca
54 Sakata Cc
55 Sakhalin, I. Ke
33 Sakhalin R. Ke
33 Sakskóbing Ef
11 Sala Ed
89 Salala Ed
26 Salamanca, Sp. Aa
89 Salamanca, U.S.A. Fc
74 Saldanha, B. Bd
61 Sale, Austral. Cc
50 Salé, Morocco Cd
44 Salem, India Dd
91 Salem, Mass. Kc
90 Salem, Oreg. Ab
84 Salem, Ore. Ab
29 Salemi Df
8 Salen Cd
21 Salerno Ed
6 Salford Ed
73 Salima Ef
91 Salina Cruz Ed
91 Salinas, Braz. Fd
91 Salinas, U.S.A. Bd
7 Salisbury, Eng. Ff

*75 Salisbury, Rhod. Ea
89 Salisbury, U.S.A. He
40 Sakhad Cc
32 Salla Eb
12 Salling, dist. Bc
84 Sallom Db
84 Salmon Db
20 Salon Cf
30 Salonta Cb
7 Salop, Co. Ee
33 Salsk Hf
21 Salsomaggiore Fe
40 Salt Bc
15 Salt L. Ac
84 Salt Lake City Db
91 Saltash Cg
8 Saltcoats Dc
12 Saltholm Fd
90 Saltillo Db
94 Salto Df
90 Salton Sea Ce
38 Saltum Bb
47 Salur Jj
21 Saluzzo Fe
92 Salvador Fd
47 Salvador, Rep. Kg
45 Salween, R. He
33 Salyany Jh
17 Salzburg Ee
16 Salzgitter Db
16 Salzwedel Db
12 Samaná I. Dd
88 Samar, I. Hj
48 Samaranda Cd
34 Samarkand Jf
20 Samassi Bc
47 Sambalpur Jh
19 Sambre, R. Dd
73 Samburu Fc
73 Samfoc Bd
88 Samnek Bd
51 Samnan Gb
66 Samoa Is. Dc
27 Sámos, I. Cb
8 Sampit, & B. Cd
51 Samshui Fd
11 Samsö, I. Dd
54 Samsun Ea
71 San, R. Ep
23 San, R. Fc
91 San Andreas, I. Bd
90 San Andres Tuxtla Ed
85 San Angelo Fc
85 San Antioco, I. Bc
85 San Antonio, I. Fc
91 San Antonio, C. Bb
†72 San Antonio do Zaire Ae
35 San Benedetto Ba
85 San Bernardino Ce
90 San Carlos Ea
93 San Carlos de Bariloche Bg
85 San Clemente, I. Ce
94 San Cristóbal, Argentina Cf
90 San Cristobal, Mexico Fd
92 San Cristóbal, Venezuela Bb
90 San Diego Ce
90 San Felipe Bf
90 San Fernando, Mexico Ec
26 San Fernando, Sp. Ab
90 San Francisco Bd
90 San Francisco de Macoris Dc
21 San Gimignano Cc
21 San Giovanni in Perseceto Ke
94 San Ignacio Cc
90 San Jorge, B. Ba
93 San Jorge, G. de Cg
94 San José, Bol. Cc
91 San José, C. Rica Be
85 San José, Phil. Db
85 San José, U.S.A. Bd
94 San Juan, Arg. Bf
91 San Juan, Par. Dc
94 San Juan, Bol. Dc
91 San Juan, Puerto Rico Ec
91 San Juan, R. Bd
91 San Julián Cg
94 San Lucas, C. Bc
93 San Luis & prov. Cf
91 San Luis Obispo Bd
90 San Luis Potosi Dc
28 San Marino, & rep. Dc
94 San Martin Cb
94 San Matias Cb
93 San Matias, G. de Cg
91 San Miguel Ad
28 San Miniato Cc
28 San Nicandro Ed
93 San Nicolas Ef

49 San Pablo Db
91 San Pedro, Cuba Ec
90 San Pedro, Mex. Db
94 San Pedro, Par. Dd
71 San Pedro, Ivory Coast Dg
91 San Pedro Sula Ad
90 San Pelice sul Panaro Ke
28 San Pietro, I. Bc
90 San Quintin Aa
93 San Rafael Cf
21 San Remo Ff
77 San Sayador Ae
91 San Salvador (Watling) I. Db
26 San Sebastián Ba
28 San Sepalcro Dc
28 San Severo Ed
9 Sarna Dd
21 Sanaga, R. Hh
43 Sanandaj (Sinneh) Fb
20 Sancerre Ab
20 Sancerrois, Collines du, mts. Ab
91 Sancti Spiritus Cb
49 Sandakan Cc
31 Sanday, I. Fa
74 Sandfish B. Ab
27 Sandikli Db
11 Sandnes Bd
50 Sandnessjöen Cb
72 Sandoa Ce
11 Sandön Cd
7 Sandown Fg
85 Sandpoint Cb
7 Sandringham He
65 Sandstone Bd
88 Sandusky Da
12 Sandvig Allinge Fa
63 Sandy C. Dc
72 Sanga, R. Bc
49 Sangihe Is. Dc
72 Sangmelina Ac
93 Sangsang Cd
72 Sangwa De
52 Sanjo Cc
72 Sankuru, R. Cd
35 Sankícar Ab
55 Sano Cc
23 Sanok Gd
8 Sanquhar Ee
94 Santa Ana, Bol. Bb
85 Santa Ana, U.S.A. Ce
94 Santa Bárbara, Brazil Dc
85 Santa Barbara, U.S.A. Ce
85 Sta. Catalina, I. Ce
95 Santa Catarina, st. Ee
91 Santa Clara, Cuba Cb
85 Santa Clara, U.S.A. Bd
94 Santa Cruz, Arg. Ch
94 Santa Cruz, Bol. Cc
68 Santa Cruz, Canary Is. Ac
85 Santa Cruz, U.S.A. Bd
94 Santa Cruz, I. Ce
93 Santa Cruz, prov. Bg
90 Santa Eugenia, Pt. Ab
94 Santa Fé, Arg. Cf
85 Santa Fé, U.S.A. Ed
94 Santa Isabel, Bolivia Cc
95 Santa Isabel, Brazil Eb
*71 Santa Isabel, Sp. Guin. Gh
21 Sta. Margherita Ligure He
95 Santa Maria Ee
94 Santa Maria, R. Ca
26 Santa Maria d'Ortiguiera Aa
94 Santa Maria da Vitória Gb
92 Santa Marta Ba
85 Santa Monica Ce
93 Santa Rosa, Arg. Cf
95 Santa Rosa, Brazil De
24 Santa Rosa, Honduras Ad
94 Santa Rosa, U.S.A. Bd
90 Santa Rosalia Bb
26 Santander Ba
26 Santarém Ba
52 Santiago, Chile Bf

* Renamed Andropov
† Renamed Russian Soviet Federative Socialist Republic

19

* Renamed St. Vincent & The Grenadines

* Renamed Harare, Zimbabwe
† Renamed Soyo

* Renamed Rey Malabo

* Renamed Shurugwi
* Renamed Emammrud
† Renamed Zvishavane
‡ Renamed Qomsheh
** Renamed Tonekabon
* Renamed Chinhoyi
† Renamed Thailand, G. of

* Renamed Namibia
* Renamed Antananarivo
† Renamed Taomasina

23

* Renamed Irian Jaya

* Renamed Mariupol'